SECRETS OF ANALYTICAL LEADERS

Other books by Wayne W. Eckerson

Performance Dashboards: Measuring, Monitoring and Managing Your Business (2005, 2010)

SECRETS

OF
ANALYTICAL
LEADERS

WAYNE W. ECKERSON

TECHNICS PUBLICATIONS, LLC

Published by:
Technics Publications, LLC
966 Woodmere Drive
Westfield, NJ 07090 U.S.A.
908-543-3050
www.TechnicsPub.com

Edited by Carol Lehn

Cover design by Mark Brye

Interior design and pagination by Glen M. Edelstein

ISBN, print ed.   978-1-9355043-4-4

First Printing 2012

Library of Congress Control Number: 2012946198

To Christina

CONTENTS

PART III. THE HARD STUFF: MANAGING DATA, ARCHITECTURE, AND TOOLS

LEVEL SETTING

DEFINITION - ANALYTICS

Analytics has two definitions. On the one hand, analytics is an umbrella term that describes the people, processes, and technologies used to turn data into insights into action. In this sense, analytics encompasses data warehousing, business intelligence (BI), performance management, and data mining.

On the other hand, the term analytics also refers to the tools and techniques for exploring data in an ad hoc fashion and generating statistical models that detect patterns and relationships in large volumes of data.

This book uses the terms "analytics" or "analytical" to refer to the first umbrella definition, and either "advanced analytics", "data mining", "statistical analysis", or "machine learning" to refer to the second definition. Chapter 2 provides more context on definitions.

DEFINITION – ANALYST

Another loaded term is "analyst". There are two basic groups of people who deliver analytical solutions. One consists of "data developers", also known as BI developers. The other consists of "analysts", who are superusers, data analysts, business analysts, statisticians, and data scientists.

Data developers work in a *top-down* environment. They produce reports and dashboards that answer mostly predefined questions, using data largely from data warehouses or data marts. In contrast, analysts work in a *bottom-up* environment. They explore data in an ad hoc fashion, using any data source.

This book delineates between the people, processes, architectures, and tools that support both top-down and bottom-up analytics. Chapters 7 to 9 differentiate the people; Chapters 10 to 12 differentiate the processes; and Chapters 16 to 18 discuss architecture and tools.

MEET THE
ANALYTICAL LEADERS

 ERIC COLSON is Chief Analytics Officer at a soon-to-be-launched internet startup. For more than 18 years, he has led data-oriented teams that span data warehousing, business intelligence, and algorithm development at companies, such as Yahoo and Netflix. Says Colson, "It's important to deliver value quickly, then evolve your designs through iteration and usage."

 DAN INGLE is Vice President of Vehicle Valuations at Kelley Blue Book, an information resource that values new and used vehicles. After overseeing the team responsible for the Kelly Blue Book's data assets and analytic applications, Ingle now oversees the group that handles vehicle valuations, which is the company's core product. "Analytics has completely changed the DNA of Kelley Blue Book. It is key to our future growth."

 TIM LEONARD recently served as Chief Technology Officer at U.S. Xpress Enterprises, the second largest privately-owned truckload carrier in the United States. Leonard helped to transform the company's IT culture and infrastructure to deliver the right information to the right people at the right time. "In my world, IT dissolves and becomes the business."

AMY O'CONNOR is Senior Director of Big Data at Nokia, the world's largest manufacturer of mobile phones. As head of the advanced analytics team, O'Connor is building a petabyte-scale analytics platform and developing a world-class team of data scientists. "Today, Nokia's raw material is data and it will form the basis of many new products and services."

KEN RUDIN is head of analytics at Facebook, where he helps the social media giant apply analytics to optimize consumer experiences and grow its business. Before that, Rudin was Vice President of Analytics and Platform Technology at Zynga, a $1 billion maker of online games. "The key is not getting the right answers; it's asking the right questions", he says.

DARREN TAYLOR is President and Chief Operating Officer at Cobalt Talon, a subsidiary of Blue Cross Blue and Shield of Kansas City (Blue KC) that offers analytic services to other healthcare companies. Taylor spent 20 years at Blue KC in various business and IT roles before helping launch the commercial service in 2012, which converted an analytical cost center to a profit center. "This has been the highlight of my career."

KURT THEARLING is Director of IT and Applied Analytics at AlixPartners LLP, a global business consulting firm. Thearling combines deep technical knowledge with a strong business sense honed by applying advanced analytical solutions in many industries. "Analytics is useless unless you curate the data and build production systems to apply your models."

ACKNOWLEDGEMENTS

A book like this isn't possible without the help of many people. I'd like to thank the analytical leaders who appear in this book: Eric Colson, Dan Ingle, Tim Leonard, Amy O'Connor, Ken Rudin, Darren Taylor, and Kurt Thearling. They spent many hours divulging their secrets of success to me, endured countless follow up questions, and spent many hours reviewing the manuscript.

I'd also like to thank the other analytical leaders whom I interviewed but who didn't make it into the book. I hope that I can write about their secrets in the next edition! They are Andrea Ballinger, Michael Linhares, Michael Masciandaro, Darrell Piatt, Oliver Ratzesberger, Bill Robinette, Robert Scanlon, Thomas Shiby, and Nick Triantos. And there are countless other analytical leaders whom I've met over the years who have graciously extended their knowledge to me but are too numerous to mention.

I am fortunate to have an energetic and innovative publisher. Steve Hoberman is a data developer of the highest order who got into the publishing business several years ago to publish his own data modeling books. He then decided to take on the book projects of several colleagues, and he has quickly demonstrated that he's a force to be reckoned with in the publishing world.

I'd also like to thank the management at TechTarget, especially Mike Bolduc and Kevin Beam, who have given me the flexibility to pursue projects like this.

Finally, I'd like to thank my wife, Christina, whose patience and understanding enabled me to steal precious family time during evenings and weekends to work on this book. I love you!

FOREWORD BY MAX FULLER

A chief responsibility for any CEO in today's business world is to build and to continually evolve the most effective strategy for mining and then leveraging the data that can make a difference within an organization. Those companies which make a significant commitment to analytics are the companies that quite often rise to become the leaders in their respective industries.

At U.S. Xpress Enterprises, we not only brought technology to the forefront of a transportation industry that had been slow to recognize its potential, but we built a structure within our organization that has allowed us to look at our business and the market in new and quite often in revolutionary ways. We are not alone.

Through analytics, companies have the ability to use information to make smarter decisions, to develop better products, to improve overall customer satisfaction and to increase profitability. Analytics can become a sustainable resource that provides a competitive advantage because it helps improve business IQ. Leveraging analytics can make companies smarter, more agile and more relevant to customers and other constituencies (including employees).

In Secrets of Analytical Leaders, Wayne Eckerson and his insightful panel of "information insiders" have assembled an important navigational tool for CEOs, CIOs and business leaders who seek to leverage the power of information. Spanning a range of industries, they demonstrate how to harness data for business gain, bridge the worlds of business and technology, and deliver remarkable solutions that give their organizations a competitive edge. The moral of the story is that when you empower the right people who empower those who work for them, you typically receive superior results.

If you are in a position of leadership within your company, you must strive to stay ahead of the changes in your industry and the markets you serve. Technology—more specifically, the use of analytics to harness information and processes—is one of the most valuable tools available to you. This book and its easy-to-follow format serve as an instructive guide for finding the best answers that can give your business a competitive advantage. For those of us seeking the key to unlock competitive advantages that will keep our businesses a step ahead, this book is highly recommended reading.

Max Fuller
CEO and Chairman of the Board
U.S. Xpress Enterprises

FOREWORD
BY MICHAEL HALBHERR

We are living in a time of radical change. From my vantage point as head of Nokia's Location and Commerce business, I see many business and technical trends shaping our future—and all depend on a new commodity: data. In our mapping business, I see the need to evolve from a road-centric tool to something that allows people to truly understand and maneuver the complexities of a modern city. To accomplish this, we need a lot of data and ways to correlate disparate information into what we call "Smart Data." Analytics is core to what we do, and how we deliver value to customers today and in the future.

I recently spoke to the Nokia board about our data, and some members questioned how we could monetize this asset. Since a few members are executives in the oil industry, I told them that data is the "oil of the future", and that you monetize this new resource the same way you monetize oil, by spending time and money refining it. In our case, we are refining data about people, locations, social interactions, traffic, musical preferences, and so on to bring maps to life.

The analytical leaders profiled in this book demonstrate how to refine data for business gain and innovation. They play a pivotal role by bridging the worlds of business and technology. When supported by the business, they've delivered remarkable solutions that have given their organizations a competitive edge.

I highly recommend this book to anyone who wants to monetize the most important resource of our time: data. It's written in language that both a CEO and a CIO can understand, and carries important lessons no matter what side of the business-technology aisle someone sits.

Michael Halbherr
Executive Vice President, Location & Commerce
Nokia

PREFACE

This book started during a conversation with Eric Colson, who was working at Netflix at the time, who said that he'd love to write a book about business intelligence and analytics. He asked if we could team up and write a book together. I thought that was a great idea because I've always admired Eric and the originality of his ideas. But as I thought about the type of book we might co-create, I realized that there are many people in our industry whose ideas and innovative approaches deserve public airing. I decided then to write a book that features multiple analytical leaders and distills their secrets to analytical success in largely their own words.

Ultimately, this book is about leadership. It's about people who create a vision for what's possible and motivate people to follow them. More specifically, it's about people who span the worlds of business and technology and help their organizations harness information for business gain. I call these leaders "purple people", and they are the real keys to analytical success. They are not "blue" in the business or "red" in technology, but a blend of both. (See the Chapter 1 for more on purple people.)

Seven leaders. The book you now have in your hands profiles seven analytical leaders from a variety of industries. In truth, I could have interviewed dozens of individuals whose work and ideas I've admired over the years, but space and time limited my scope. So, I decided to select individuals who run an end-to-end analytics program. By that, I mean they oversee teams that span the full range of analytical activities, from data warehousing and business intelligence to performance management and advanced analytics to platforms and data infrastructure. Moreover, I selected analytical leaders who are quintessential "purple people"—organizational catalysts who make it possible to turn data into insights into action.

I conducted several interviews with each analytical leader, totaling four to five hours in length. During the first interview, I asked them to discuss three or four things that have been critical to their success in running an analytics program. Their keys to success are summarized in Chapter 5, and then explained in more detail in subsequent chapters of the book. During additional interviews, I plumbed the leaders' personal backgrounds and asked questions that people typically ask me about analytics. Those questions became the basis for the 20 chapters in this book. I subsequently transcribed, paraphrased, and parsed each leader's comments and placed them in the appropriate chapters. Some analytical leaders provide the content for all or most of a chapter because of the originality of their ideas or their unique skills among the group. Conversely, not every leader commented on every topic, so all seven are not represented in each chapter.

Departures. One of the challenges in writing a book like this is that time gets in the way. The process has taken nearly a year, which is six months longer than I anticipated. (I thought this format would be easy!) During the additional six months, four of the analytical leaders profiled in this book left their companies (Tim Leonard, Eric Colson, Kurt Thearling, and Ken Rudin) and two were promoted into business-focused jobs (Dan Ingle and Darren Taylor), leaving Amy O'Connor as my only constant. (However, Amy started her current position three months before I commenced this project!) The moral of this story—besides the necessity of hitting deadlines—is that talented analytical leaders are in high demand and continually seek new challenges, so they don't stay long in one place!

How to read this book. The chapters in this book are generally short and self-contained, so you can read this book in short gulps or jump to topics that interest you most without losing context. However, the chapters are logically sequenced so business and technical executives can step through the process of implementing an analytics program. *Part I* introduces the seven analytical leaders and defines what analytics is and why it's valuable, among other things. *Part II* discusses the "soft stuff": how to manage the people, processes, and projects involved in delivering analytical solutions. And *Part III* focuses on the "hard stuff": the architecture, technology, and tools that comprise an analytical ecosystem.

At the beginning of each chapter, I summarize the ideas of the analytical leaders on the topic and then provide contextual background based on my 20+ years in the field. My commentary frames the ensuing discussion or tackles topics that the analytical leaders didn't address. In many ways, this book is a print version of a panel discussion in which a moderator frames a topic and then guides the conversation among panelists.

If you want an executive summary of the entire book, read Chapter 5. This chapter presents my framework for analytical success and summarizes each analytical leader's keys to running a successful analytics program. Subsequent chapters explore these ideas and themes in greater detail.

WHO SHOULD READ THIS BOOK?

This book is geared to business and technology executives who want to understand best practices for starting and managing an analytics programs and how to deliver high-impact analytical solutions. On the business side, this includes top executives and business unit heads who sponsor analytics programs. On the technical side, it includes directors of analytics and heads of business intelligence and data warehousing who want to learn from fellow practitioners and discover tips and techniques for taking their analytics' programs to the next level.

The book is also relevant to the staff of business and technical executives. On the business side, the book helps business analysts, statisticians, and data scientists better understand their roles in the data-to-insights-to-action workflow. On the technical side, data architects, developers, administrators, and trainers learn the secrets of how high-performance business intelligence and data warehousing (BI/DW) teams are organized and deliver value. Finally, the book appeals to consultants and academics who will find useful frameworks and anecdotes to share with clients or in the classroom.

My hope is that readers will find this book both a handy reference and an inspirational guide to shape both their approach to analytics and their analytical careers.

PART 1

SETTING THE STAGE

CHAPTER 1

WHAT IS AN ANALYTICAL LEADER?

ANALYTICS REQUIRES "PURPLE PEOPLE"

Breakthrough innovation occurs when reconciling opposites. Living at one end or the other of a philosophical or cultural spectrum is comfortable, but not terribly interesting or instructive. You know the answers before people ask the questions. Your past, present, and future are hard wired and unchanging.

But people who live at the confluence of disparate approaches and opinions have a broader perspective. They see connections and possibilities that others miss. They speak multiple languages and gracefully move between different groups and norms. They continuously translate, synthesize, and unify. As a result, they imagine new ways to solve old problems, and they reinvent old ways to tackle new challenges. They are powerful change agents and value creators.

In the world of analytics, I call these men and women "purple people". They are not "blue" in the business or "red" in technology, but a blend of the two, hence purple. Purple people are true analytical leaders, and they are the central focus of this book.

STRADDLING TWO WORLDS

In many organizations, business people and technologists move in different circles. There is a yawning cultural gulf between them: they speak different languages, report to different managers, socialize with different people, and have different career ambitions. Neither side trusts or particularly respects the other. Neither side understands the pressures, deadlines, and challenges the other faces. They are at loggerheads. Only "purple people" can break this logjam.

Analytics is not like most information technology (IT) disciplines; it requires a thorough and ongoing understanding of business issues, processes, tactics, and strategies to succeed. Analytics is about delivering information that answers business questions and tests business assumptions and hypotheses. And since those questions and hypotheses are shaped by market conditions, they change continuously. As a result, an analytical solution can't succeed unless it continuously adapts to an ever-changing business environment.

The only way to create an adaptable system—an intrinsic contradiction—is to find people who are comfortable straddling the worlds of business and technology. Purple people can speak the language of business and translate requirements into terms that technologists can understand. Conversely, they can show business people the latent value of data and how to exploit it through judicious investments in people, process, and analytical technologies. Because purple people move comfortably in both camps, they serve as data ambassadors who reconcile business and IT and forge a strong and lasting partnership that delivers true business value.

WHERE DO YOU FIND PURPLE PEOPLE?

The best analytical leaders are proverbial switch hitters. They have strong credentials and a solid reputation in either a business or technology discipline—and then they switch sides. This versatility creates an immediate impact and is a key attribute of a purple person. The analytical leaders profiled in this book exhibit this versatility.

For example, Ken Rudin was a product marketer and software

entrepreneur prior to landing the position of director of analytics at Zynga and, and more recently, Facebook. Dan Ingle, who was a business consultant before running Kelley Blue Book's data acquisition and business intelligence (BI) teams, now runs the company's vehicle valuations team on the business side. Darren Taylor started out as a business analyst at Blue KC before leading a series of systems development and data warehousing projects in the IT department. He then moved back to the business to manage the analytics program that he helped convert into a commercial operation, which he now manages as president and COO.

Some technologists never relinquish their technology roles, but gravitate to the business side of analytics in order to get things done. Tim Leonard, chief technology officer at U.S. Xpress, learned to talk the language of business to gain the credibility and trust that cleared the way for him to implement several successful analytical solutions. Kurt Thearling applied his statistical and machine learning skills as a business consultant to help companies generate business value from analytical tools. Amy O'Connor balanced her technology credentials with a master's degree in business administration which helped her earn the top "big data" job at Nokia.

Recruiting others. Astute analytical leaders recruit other purple people to serve on their teams. They place a premium on people who have strong business experience, high emotional IQ, and an innate curiosity and passion for data. Although analytical leaders require candidates to possess strong technical skills, including familiarity with statistical concepts, they say it's just as important that they understand the business, know how to communicate with others, and work effectively in a team.

Analytical leaders love to hire technically savvy business people. When marketing or financial professionals, for example, join an analytical team, they bring knowledge of business people, processes, and challenges in their departments, and this instantly improves communication. For example, business converts can speak honestly with former colleagues when hashing out issues and clarifying requirements. They know the difference between "needs" and "wishes" and can help create a realistic priority list that works for both sides. In short, they serve as liaisons, becoming the glue that binds business and technology teams together.

An infusion of purple. In truth, successful analytical leaders need purple people at all levels of the organization, from the CEO down to the entry level developer and analyst. As we'll see in Chapter 6, top executives can make or break an analytics program. Those who invest in fact-based decision making and performance measurement processes create analytically-driven organizations that use data to deliver value. And in Chapters 8 and 10, we'll see how developers and analysts who sit side by side with the business people they support become integral members of those teams. By gathering requirements directly, developers and analysts learn the business inside and out and deliver better solutions faster.

People often ask me how to advance their career in the analytics field. The answer is obvious: become a purple person. By straddling business and technology, you can become an indispensable change agent who leverages technology to deliver business-critical solutions. The analytical leaders profiled in this book testify to the power of "going purple".

MEET YOUR ANALYTICAL LEADERS

ERIC COLSON

EDUCATION:
MS, Management Science & Engineering,
Stanford University (in progress)
MS, Information Systems, Golden Gate University
BA, Economics, San Francisco State

CURRENT WORK:
Chief Data Officer, Undisclosed Internet startup

PAST WORK:
VP of Data Science and Engineering, Netflix
Manager of Business Intelligence, Yahoo
Product Manager, Blue Martini Software Consultant,
Business Intelligence and Data Warehousing, Proxicom
Advanced Analytics, Information Resources, Inc.
Marketing Statistician, F.W. Woolworth

Eric Colson, 40, is Chief Analytics Officer at a soon-to-be-launched internet startup that he joined in August, 2012 after working at Netflix for six years, most recently as Vice President of Data Science and Engineering. In that capacity, he led a team of 80 people, spanning business intelligence, data science platforms, experimentation, and machine learning/algorithms. Despite the array of technology under his purview, Colson says the most critical tools in his arsenal are autonomy and context. By that he means embedding developers in business units and empowering each of them to build complete analytical solutions on their own.

In a dynamic, fast-paced business, change is constant and speed is paramount. Managing data in such a hyper-paced environment requires creative, out-of-the-box thinking. "It is important to experiment, learn fast, and continually change your analytical environment," says Colson. "There is no place for rigid processes; you need to keep things fluid and rely on the good judgment of your people, rather than impose strict rules."

Surviving and thriving in this crucible of change has turned Colson into a data philosopher of sorts. He uses terms like "spanner", "eventually cohesive", and "punctuated change" to describe his agile approach to application development and architectural design. And he uses references from Adam Smith and Charles Darwin to describe how data warehousing architectures can naturally evolve with the business.

Although quite cerebral, Colson is a pragmatist at heart. As an undergraduate economics major, Colson was enthralled by the curvilinear models that depicted optimal business states. But when he entered the business world, he discovered that companies couldn't draw such lines because the data didn't exist or wasn't in a suitable condition to support analysis. That experience catapulted Colson into the data side of business. "I've been on a quest for perfect analytics for 20 years, and data warehousing, business intelligence, and analytics have been a means to that end," he says.

DAN INGLE

EDUCATION:
BA, Management Information Systems,
Ohio State University

CURRENT WORK:
VP, Vehicle Valuations, Kelley Blue Book

PAST WORK:
SVP, Analytic Insights & Technology, Kelley Blue Book
Director of IT, Capital One Auto Finance
VP, Data Services, PeopleFirst.com
Project Lead, Thomsen Technology Consulting Group
Project Lead, James Martin & Company
Consultant, Ernst & Young

Dan Ingle, 42, is Vice President of Vehicle Valuations at Kelley Blue Book, an information resource for new and used automobile values and related content that several years ago embraced analytics as a strategic capability to compete in an increasingly volatile and competitive information services market. "Analytics has completely changed the DNA of Kelley Blue Book," says Ingle, who was a key driver in the company's transformation.

Although Kelley Blue Book hired Ingle to migrate the 500-person company to a modern technology platform, he took the opportunity to help orchestrate the implementation of an analytics infrastructure that has reinvented the firm's car valuation process. Rather than estimate values based on samples and intuition, Kelley Blue Book now runs sophisticated forecasting models against ever-increasing volumes of automobile transactions, delivering more relevant values, more frequently, and with greater granularity. With his background in developing large-scale, data-centric applications, including several data warehouses, Ingle was the right man at the right place at the right time to help elevate Kelley Blue Book's analytical game.

From the get go, Ingle has combined technical knowledge with business savvy. He began managing large-scale IT projects for Ernst & Young as a newly minted college graduate. "It was a sink or swim environment," says Ingle, "but the best career move I ever made. At a young age, I got to work closely with business people and manage large, strategic business-technology projects."

And Ingle has been swimming ever since. As an endurance athlete, Ingle has competed in six Ironman contests, including two in Hawaii that are the triathlon equivalent of the Super Bowl. He believes the attributes required to succeed in an endurance race are the same for managing a successful analytics program. "You have to work hard, stay focused, and not get distracted by things you can't control," he says. "And you have to be consistent week in and out and bounce back quickly from setbacks."

TIM LEONARD

EDUCATION:
BA, Information Management,
Colorado Tech University (in process)

PAST WORK:
Chief Technology Officer and VP, U.S. Xpress Enterprises
Senior Manager of BI, Dell
Director of Information Mgmt, AT&T
U.S. Army Military Intelligence

Tim Leonard, 45, served as the Chief Technology Officer at U.S. Xpress Enterprises, a mid-size trucking company based in Chattanooga, Tennessee, from 2009 to 2012.Leonard is a take-charge data professional whose primary desire is to use data to transform organizations. During his tenure at U.S. Xpress, Leonard did just that, implementing dozens of new applications and systems and overhauling the data warehouse, which now provides an integrated view of all U.S. Xpress operations.

In 2012, Leonard's team rebuilt a fleet management system that delivers near real-time data to regional fleet managers so they can optimize the carrying capacity and profits of their trucks. Called XPM, this near real-time, mobile, operational BI application became the technical underpinning of a new business strategy to realign the company's operations. "We used data to restructure our operations center and give the company a competitive edge," says Leonard.

Leonard is no stranger to taking on tough challenges. He cut his "data teeth" in the First Gulf War where he was a military intelligence analyst reporting to Army Central Command (ARCENT), and then to CENTCOM Commander to General Norman Schwarzkopf. "I was the eyes and ears of the General during the war," says Leonard. As part of his job, Leonard put together "electronic orders of battle" (EOB)—in essence, glorified data marts—that combined field and electronic intelligence. If the generals gave an order to destroy enemy radar, for example, officers used Leonard's EOB data mart to pinpoint enemy defenses and design a battle plan. "People used our data to plan attacks on the enemy—it was a matter of life and death," says Leonard, a winner of the Bronze Star. "That's how I learned that data

AMY O'CONNOR

EDUCATION:
MBA, Northeastern University
MS, Engineering, University of Connecticut

CURRENT WORK:
Senior Director of Big Data, Nokia

Past Work:
Social Media Marketing, Angel Charitable Trust
Senior Director Cloud Services Product Mgmt, Nokia
VP, Services Marketing, Sun Microsystems
Director, Program Management, Toysmart
Director, Program Management, GTE Internetworking

Amy O'Connor is Senior Director of Big Data at Nokia, one of the world's largest providers of mobile devices and internet services for untethered consumers. With an engineer's eye for detail and marketer's sense of the big picture, O'Connor is responsible for pulling together Nokia's vast and far-flung stores of data into a single repository that creative people across the company can mine to better understand consumer behavior and create new information products and services.

One of the first things O'Connor did upon arriving at Nokia was to take an inventory of data throughout the company to understand what existed, where it was located, and what was being thrown away. O'Connor is now building a central data repository on Apache Hadoop to store both log data from Nokia's numerous Web sites, and streaming device data from more than 1.3 billion Nokia mobile phones worldwide. Finally, O'Connor is fortifying the company's analytical capabilities by hiring data scientists to mine the repository of consumer-driven data.

O'Connor is the perfect candidate to help Nokia achieve its strategic vision of profiting from data. She has a strong technical background in computer science, electrical engineering, and corporate storage systems that is balanced with marketing savvy she honed while a product manager and social media maven. "Before I joined Nokia, I was looking for an opportunity in big data, social networking, mobility, or cloud services. Nokia has hooks into all of these areas, which makes it an exciting place to work. It has a big vision for data and analytics," she says.

KEN RUDIN

EDUCATION:
MBA, Stanford University
BA, Harvard University

CURRENT WORK:
Director of Analytics, Facebook

PAST WORK:
VP of Analytics and Platform Technologies, Zynga
Founder, CEO, and CMO, LucidEra
VP and GM, Siebel CRM on Demand, Siebel Systems
VP Marketing, Siebel Analytics, Siebel Systems
SVP Products and Engineering, Salesforce.com
Founder and CEO, Emergent Corporation
GM, Data Warehousing and Parallel Systems, Oracle
Group Product Manager, Programming Tools, Oracle

Ken Rudin, 46, is Director of Analytics at Facebook, where he helps the social media giant apply analytics to optimize consumer experiences and grow its business. Before that (and during the creation of this book), Rudin was Vice President of Analytics and Platform Technology at Zynga, a $1 billion maker of online games, such as Farmville and Mafia Wars, where he oversaw the analytics and data warehousing teams as well as the data and communications components of the company's core gaming infrastructure.

Rudin's youthful good looks belie a long and distinguished career in the software industry. He helped inaugurate the era of software-as-a-service (SaaS) at Salesforce.com and Siebel Systems, and founded two companies: LucidEra, an early business intelligence SaaS company, which he ran before coming to Zynga, and a consulting firm, Emergent Corporation, which specialized in large-scale data warehousing solutions. However, Rudin says his biggest accomplishment was helping Zynga CEO Mark Pincus achieve his vision of marrying art and science to dominate the online gaming industry. "Rather than designing games solely by intuition, Zynga couples great game designers with superb product managers and analysts and constantly measures what works and doesn't work," he says. "This revolutionary approach is instrumental to Zynga's success."

Rudin is not your typical analytics director. He brings a strong software marketing background to the practice of analytics and his insights are as pragmatic as they are unconventional. Rudin thinks outside the box and is not afraid to buck conventional wisdom. Moreover, he has the credibility and leadership skills to get others to follow him. His ability to span technology and business gives him unique insights about how to deliver value from analytics. As a result, many analytical teams in Silicon Valley turn to Rudin for advice.

DARREN TAYLOR

EDUCATION:
MBA, Baker University
BA, Truman State University

CURRENT WORK:
President and COO, Cobalt Talon

PAST WORK:
20 years with Blue Cross Blue Shield of Kansas City:
-VP, Enterprise Analytics and Data Mangement
-VP, Integrated Data Systems
-AVP, Healthcare Information Services
-Director, System Conversion Team
-Provider Contracting and Reimbursement Specialist

Darren Taylor, 42, is President and Chief Operating Officer of Cobalt Talon, a subsidiary of Blue Cross and Blue Shield of Kansas City (Blue KC) that offers data management and analytical solutions to other healthcare companies. Taylor is the classic "purple person", having held positions in both business and information technology at Blue KC, a mid-size health insurer serving approximately one million members. During his 20-year tenure at Blue KC, Taylor served as director of a medical economics unit; oversaw a large portion of the company's Year 2000 systems consolidation project; overhauled the corporate data warehouse; and ran the company's analytics program, which he now manages as a commercial enterprise. "One of the keys to my success," says Taylor, "is that as a business analyst early in my career, I gained a broad perspective on the business, which subsequently enabled me to connect the dots between business and IT."

Taylor's BI team has received many accolades. It has twice won the Best Practices Awards from The Data Warehousing Institute and ComputerWorld Magazine, and on multiple occasions has garnered his company's Partnership Award, the Strategic Business Project award, and the prestigious President's Award.

However, Taylor's biggest accomplishment is leading a talented team that transformed the company's data warehouse from a cost center to a profit center. This rare accomplishment began in 2003 when his team rebuilt the corporate data warehouse, and then gained momentum in 2010 when his team created an analytical infrastructure that runs a consolidated set of analytical models and applications. Today, under Taylor's leadership, Blue KC offers its data warehousing and analytical infrastructure as a commercial offering to other healthcare companies. "I've never been more excited, because there is so much opportunity in the healthcare space for this type of solution," he says.

KURT THEARLING

EDUCATION:
PhD, Electrical Engineering, University of Illinois
BS, Computer and Electrical Engineering,
University of Michigan

CURRENT WORK:
Head of Decision Sciences, Vertex Business Services

PAST WORK:
VP, Strategic Technology, Capital One
Director of Engineering, AnVil
Chief Scientist, Wheelhouse
Director of Analytics, Exchange Software
Senior Scientist, Dun & Bradstreet
Senior Scientist, Thinking Machines

Kurt Thearling, 48, is Director of IT and Applied Analytics at AlixPartners LLP, a global business consulting firm. Thearling combines deep technical knowledge with a strong business sense honed by applying advanced analytical solutions in a variety of industries.

Thearling has prodigious technical knowledge. He earned a PhD in electrical engineering from the University of Illinois, where he also studied machine learning and artificial intelligence. In his first job out of school at Thinking Machines in Cambridge, Massachusetts, Thearling developed Darwin, one of the first commercial data mining tools, which ran on the company's supercomputers. Later, at Exchange Applications, Thearling helped build a deployment platform that integrated analytics and customer relationship management tools to help marketing profes-sionals better target customers and measure campaign effectiveness. And at Capital One, he drove the development of a production infra-structure that automated the creation and deployment of analytical models. Thearling also holds multiple patents and has served on advisory boards for various data mining companies, including SAS Institute.

Like any good data scientist, Thearling has an insatiable curiosity. Throughout his 20-year career, he has continually sought new indus-tries and business contexts in which to apply his statistical and analytical skills. But Thearling is not just a pure technologist; he has always gravitated to the practical application of statistical techniques and tools. He says he "specializes in delivering value at the intersection of analytics and business. Today, Thearling enjoys helping companies increase their analytical capabilities and develop the appropriate data and analytical infrastructure to scale their analytical activities. "Over the next decade, the use of analytics will increase dramatically across many industries, creating opportunities for those with the right skills and experience," he says.

SUMMARY

The analytical leaders profiled in this book are proverbial "purple people": they are a perfect blend of business and technology. All started in the technology field, but quickly gravitated to leadership positions in which they were held accountable for applying technology to business issues. Their versatility enabled them to bridge these two diverse worlds and deliver value-added business solutions.

Given their position at the top of the analytics food chain, the analytical leaders have a unique view of this data-driven discipline. However, the next chapter puts them to the test, asking for a universal definition of analytics. This is easier said than done, since analytics means different things to different people.

CHAPTER 2:

WHAT IS ANALYTICS?

When asked to define analytics, most of the analytical leaders profiled in this book hesitated before answering. None really had a clear, crisp definition at hand. After some thought, most supplied a couple of definitions, which were surprisingly consistent. On the one hand, they defined analytics broadly, as the entire technology ecosystem that delivers actionable insights to decision makers. On the other, they defined it narrowly, as advanced analytical technologies and processes that statisticians and data scientists use to tease patterns out of data. Interestingly, most underscored the importance of a data warehouse to running an effective analytics program.

As an industry analyst, part of my job is to define new technologies and markets so consumers can make smart buying decisions. This is tougher to do than it sounds, which is why our analytical leaders struggled here. Like most commonly used words, analytics is a slippery term. It means different things to different people. What I've discovered after 20+ years in the business is that every major buzzword has two primary dimensions: an industry dimension and a technology dimension. The way people define analytics depends on the dimension to which they're referring.

Given this context, I define analytics with a capital "A" as an umbrella term that represents industry trends, and analytics with a small "a" as the technologies to analyze data.

ANALYTICS WITH A CAPITAL "A"

Analytics, as an umbrella term, describes the people, processes, and technologies that turn data into insights that drive business decisions and actions. Interestingly, I used the same definition to describe data warehousing in 1995, business intelligence in 2000, and performance management in 2005. (See Figure 2-1.) Although the terms have changed as the technology has advanced, our basic objective has remained the same for the past 20 years: use data to make smarter decisions.

FIGURE 2-1. EVOLUTION OF ANALYTICS

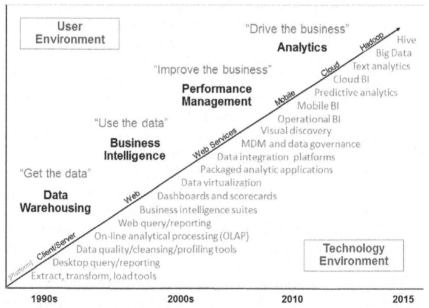

The process of turning data to insights to action has been called many things over the past 20 years and supported by many different technologies. The pace of innovation in this field shows no sign of diminishing.

During the past 20 years, there have been various umbrella terms that describe what we now call analytics. Each new buzzword represents an evolutionary step toward the goal of using data to make smarter decisions. And each step applies new methodologies and technologies to address real-world business issues.

Many people today use the term analytics as a proxy for everything required to "turn data into insights into action." The most prominent person who defines analytics this way is Tom Davenport, whose *Harvard Business Review* articles and books on the subject have prompted many executives to pursue analytics as a sustainable source of competitive advantage. Davenport is savvy enough to know that if he had called his book "Competing on Business Intelligence" instead of "Competing on Analytics", he would not have received the same traction for his concepts. That's because business intelligence is an older umbrella term that has fallen out of favor and now carries an information technology (IT) connotation. (I personally still prefer the term "business intelligence" because it perfectly describes what we do: use information to make the business run more intelligently.)

Thanks to Davenport's work, many executives have gotten "religion" about analytics. They want to go from "analytical laggard" to an "analytical competitor" in one fell swoop. Many think that all they need to do is hire an expert, buy a tool, and kick off a project. Although this might buy short-term relief, it doesn't deliver sustainable business value. An organization that wants to do analytics with a capital "A", realistically must first master data warehousing, business intelligence, and performance measurement. Analytics, like life, is evolutionary; you must pass through all the phases before you achieve the desired end state. Fortunately, given the collective knowledge we've gained in the past 20 years, it's possible for an organization to accelerate through these phases much faster than it could previously if it has the right funding, expertise, and executive commitment.

ANALYTICS WITH A SMALL "A"

From a technology perspective, analytics with a small "a" describes the technologies and techniques that business people use to analyze data. Analytical technology is a big tent. It spans everything from dashboards and visual analysis tools to statistics and machine learning.

There are two major categories of tools: reporting tools and analysis tools. Reporting tools, which include dashboards and scorecards, enable users to monitor key metrics and get answers to predefined questions. Analysis tools, on the other hand, enable users to explore data in an ad hoc fashion to discover patterns, trends, and anomalies. Generally speaking, business people use reporting tools to monitor data, and analysis tools to explore it.

During the past 20 years, there have been two waves of reporting tools and two waves of analysis tools. (See Figure 2-2.) Each successive wave provides greater business value and delivers additional insight. Reporting tools enable users to monitor business metrics. They generally meet the information needs of casual users—people who use information to do their jobs. Analysis tools enable users to explore data in an ad hoc fashion. They generally serve the needs of power users, people who are paid to analyze data.

FIGURE 2-2. WAVES OF REPORTING AND ANALYSIS

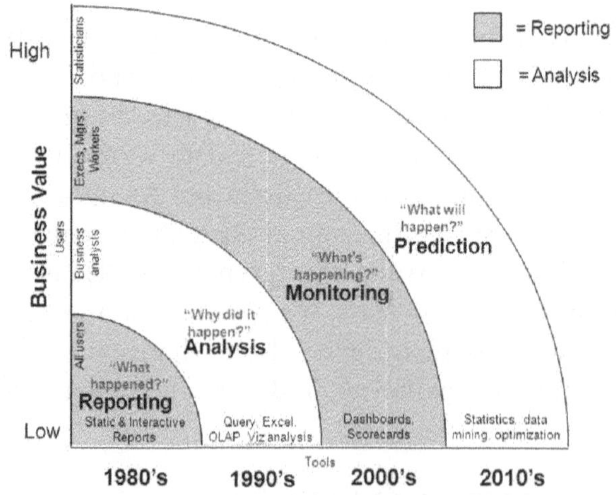

Analytical tools have evolved in phases, alternating between reporting tools and analysis tools. Reporting tools enable users to monitor business metrics, while analysis tools enable users to explore data in an ad hoc fashion.

Interestingly, each wave of reporting has been followed by a wave of analysis. It's as if reporting and analysis are two celestial bodies that orbit each other in a perpetual embrace. In reality, reporting and analysis are two distinct, but inter-related, disciplines that organizations must master to succeed with analytics. Companies that harmonize reporting and analysis in a single analytical ecosystem often deliver breakthrough performance. (See Chapter 17 for more on analytical ecosystems.)

WAVES OF REPORTING

The first wave of reporting helps business users understand "what happened" in the past (e.g., yesterday, last week, or last month), while the second wave monitors "what is happening now". The first wave generally delivers detailed static reports to users via email or print, while the second wave delivers performance dashboards. The major difference is that a report gives you all the detail at once, while a dashboard graphically illustrates the performance of key metrics and parcels out remaining information on demand.

A well designed dashboard enables users to quickly visualize performance and then navigate to the details, if needed. It consists of three layers that correspond to the first three waves of analytics described above: monitor, analyze, and drill to detail (MAD).[1] (See Figure 2-3.) The top layer displays a handful of metrics in graphical form, usually as stoplights or charts; the second layer provides filters that let users analyze the root cause of an issue using dimensional data sets; and the third level provides detailed data in a report or list form. In essence, a dashboard is a visual exception report that displays critical data at a glance, but gives users access to any data they need in three clicks or less. MAD dashboards are intuitive to use and conform to the way most business users want to consume information.

---

1   See my book, *Performance Dashboards: Measuring, Monitoring, and Managing Your Business* for a more detailed description of the MAD framework for designing dashboards and scorecards.

FIGURE 2-3. THE MAD DASHBOARD FRAMEWORK

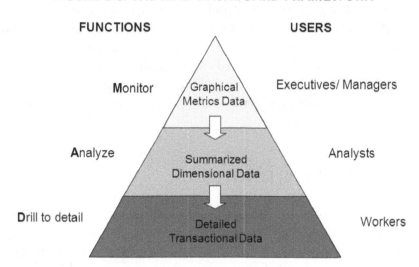

The MAD framework depicts how to design a layered, performance dashboard that gives all users a graphical view of top-level metrics and three-click access to any data.

Most performance dashboards consist of about 10 top-level metrics and 12 to 20 dimensions focused on a single business area. This creates a nice-sized information sandbox that is big enough to answer 60% to 80% of the questions business users might ask about a particular subject, but small enough so they don't get lost in the data. It's also an ideal size to ensure optimal performance since dashboard displays often consist of dozens or more queries. Furthermore, it enables administrators to tailor dashboards to individual roles and departments, so users only see the metrics and data that are relevant to them. In a well-designed dashboard, every pixel counts.

WAVES OF ANALYSIS

Like reporting, there have been two waves of analysis. The first wave addresses the question, "Why did it happen?" while the second wave answers, "What will happen?" Technically speaking, the first wave uses deductive analysis, and the second wave uses inductive analysis.

Deductive Analysis. With deductive analysis, business users explore a hypothesis. They take an educated guess about what might be at the root cause of some anomaly or performance alert and then use any number of analytical tools to explore the data to either verify or negate their hypothesis. If the hypothesis proves false, they come up with a new hypothesis and repeat the process. Analysts often use Excel, SQL, ad hoc query tools, and visual discovery tools to perform deductive analytics.

Inductive Analysis. Inductive analysis is the opposite. Business users don't start with a hypothesis, they start with a business outcome or goal, such as: "Find the top 10% of our customers and prospects who are most likely to respond to this offer." To answer this question, they gather relevant historical data and apply statistical or machine learning algorithms to the data. In other words, they don't start with a hypothesis; they start with an objective and a set of data and let the algorithms discover the patterns and anomalies for them.

In truth, there is a lot of deductive thinking required to create machine learning models, as we'll discover in Chapters 8 and 13. Skilled analytical modelers have a sixth sense about what data to gather, which variables to select, and how to format the data to achieve the highest degree of model accuracy. Such analytical "intuition" comes from years of creating models, along with a deep understanding of the business domain and available data. As several analytical leaders mention later in this book, creating accurate models that deliver business value requires a combination of art and science.

So, in the end, there is no simple or singular definition of analytics. At best, there are two definitions, one which corresponds to the overall goal of turning data into insights into action, and a second, which refers to the technologies required to achieve that goal.

COMMENTARY FROM ANALYTICAL LEADERS

LEONARD: Like Wayne says, analytics refers to the processes, technologies, and best practices that turn data into information and knowledge that drives optimal business decisions and actions. It is about using data to answer business questions that save the company money or increase revenue, as well as identify patterns, trends, and relationships in the data that have business significance. Sometimes, analytics uses more complex mathematical techniques than simple reporting to solve business problems.

All this used to happen within the IT department, but, at U.S. Xpress, we moved all the ad hoc reporting and analysis to the business where possible. We trained business analysts in each department how to build their own reports and dashboards. They often can build these dashboards in less than a day because we made it easy for them to access data in the data warehouse. This freed our IT team to focus on provisioning data and adapting the information infrastructure to the near real-time, mobile requirements of a shipping company.

THEARLING: Broadly, I think of analytics as the process of extracting meaningful patterns from data. You can do this by squinting your eyes at a dense spreadsheet, reading a report or dashboard, or working with a statistician to craft a complex model using R or SAS. The word "meaningful" is important here. The pattern or insight must be statistically valid and valuable to the business. People are good at finding patterns in data, but sometimes those patterns are just coincidences.

But, analytics is not just about exploring data and finding insights. It's also about operationalizing those insights. For instance, a bank discovers through analysis that it needs to lower credit limits to maintain optimal risk levels. That's a nice insight but has no value unless someone acts on it. But how do you change credit limits on millions of accounts? Sometimes finding insights is a lot easier than putting them into production.

TAYLOR: I view analytics as a discovery process where people find previously unknown trends and insights that can positively impact the business. The analytical process doesn't necessarily have to be sophisticated. You don't necessarily need advanced tools or a PhD in statistics to make a break-through discovery. Sometimes a valuable insight happens when someone looks at a set of data for the first time. A blend of basic and advanced analytical approaches often leads to the most actionable outcomes.

Creating a true analytical culture is 80% of the challenge we face. Traditionally, we have been a report-writing culture in which people depend on others to get information for them. We are now focused on flipping that around and demon-strating that everyone can explore data on their own with the tools we've given them. This is happening, but we must educate people at all levels of the organi-zation and demonstrate business results.

O'CONNOR: Analytics is the process of turning data into something of value. Although Nokia does traditional business intelligence and data warehousing, today it is heavily focused on using advanced analytics to develop a new understanding of how people want to interact with the physical world. We believe that the mobile market is moving into its third wave, in which the physical and online worlds blur.

Nokia's continued investment in location services through our subsidiary, NavTeq, means that we have activity data from a wide range of sensors found on and around us: geographical positioning systems (GPS), Bluetooth, near-field communications (NFC), and WiFi. But it's not enough to simply collect a trillion data points about the physical world, you have to turn them into knowledge. So we combine reference data we know about the world—every street, public transport schedule, and traffic blackspot—with human and other activities—places searched, routes requested, traffic flows, and weather events.

Nokia uses analytical models and tools to combine reference and activity data, creating what we call "smart data". And this data, delivered via analytics, enables us to develop new business models, products, and services. For us, analytics is moving beyond business transparency and decision support to business and product innovation.

RUDIN: There are two types of analyses, one is basic, and the other advanced. Basic analysis provides insights into current business operations and helps optimize existing processes. We use this type of analysis to discover how well things are working. On the other hand, advanced analytics helps identify new opportunities and innovative things to do, such as devising new ways to target customers or personalize their experiences on the Web. This type of analysis addresses more complex questions and uses more advanced techniques, such as classification and regressions.

I think of analytics more as a process than a series of tools. People start with basic reporting and then move into analysis and then data mining. Reporting helps them understand what happened, analytics why it happened, and data mining what will happen next. Analytics is also a data pipeline. You collect, standardize, integrate, clean, deliver, and then analyze the data. It's a data factory that delivers insights that optimize the way you run your business.

INGLE: Analytics is the latest in a string of industry buzzwords that attempt to frame what we do at Kelley Blue Book. It's the art and science of aligning the right people, processes, and technologies to turn data into information and actionable insights. At Kelley Blue Book, analytics powers our products and our trusted brand. Our vehicle valuations are analytical artifacts. We also use analytics to drive internal decisions and actions in our business. Analytics is both key to what we do and how we do it. It's safe to say that Kelley Blue Book has fully embraced analytics.

Data warehousing is the foundation for analytics. It provides clean, consistent, integrated, and accurate data that people can analyze. Business intelligence consists of the reporting and dashboard tools that turn data into information and drive business decisions and actions. Analytics also refers to predictive modeling that creates our forecasts and valuations. For example, we use linear regressions to forecast vehicle values and purchasing trends. We also use analytical models to estimate our Web site traffic and optimize our advertising spending.

 **COLSON:** Analytics is the use of data and quantitative techniques to discover and apply new knowledge about customers, products, and services. In some cases, business users discover knowledge through self-service query and reporting tools, otherwise known as business intelligence tools. In other cases, they collaborate with data scientists who use advanced statistical methods, such as regression, clustering, support vector machines, to discover hidden patterns in data and test business hypotheses.

Companies apply this knowledge in many ways. At a strategic level, analytics gives companies greater visibility into customer preferences, markets, and other things. At a more detailed level, companies use analytics to help design products and services and automate decisions by embedding algorithms in operational applications.

Analytics spans many data management and analysis tasks: data acquisition, data processing, data warehousing, data modeling, business intelligence, experimentation, machine learning, algorithm design, and product engineering. These functions can all fit under the umbrella term, "analytics". But it is important not to focus on the functions—they are simply a means to an end—the key is to focus on the business.

SUMMARY

Although the term "analytics" may defy exact definition, in common parlance, it has two meanings: Analytics with a capital "A" is an umbrella term that represents the entire analytical ecosystem needed to turn data into actions; and analytics with a small "a" consists of reporting and analysis tools that enable business users to track performance and detect patterns in data. Despite its semantic slipperiness, analytics is much easier to define than deploy, as the next chapter on analytical IQ illustrates.

CHAPTER 3

WHAT IS YOUR ANALYTICS IQ?

MATURITY MODELS

Chapter 2 described the evolution of analytics during the past 20 years. You might think that 20 years is enough time for every medium- and large-sized organization to develop a mature analytical practice, but it isn't. Most organizations struggle when it comes to implementing a full-fledged analytics program. Overall, the analytical IQ of most organizations today is middling to low.

Competing on Analytics. In their book *Analytics at Work*, authors Tom Davenport, Jeanne Harris, and Robert Morison present a five-stage maturity model for analytics. (See Figure 3-1.) When I speak in public and ask people to assess the maturity of their organizations based on this model, most say they are at stage two or three. In other words, they've started their analytical journeys but have yet to make significant headway. But they are quick to note that they want to be at level four or five in a few years. They understand the value of analytics and see it as a competitive differentiator, even though they may not be quite sure how to implement it.

FIGURE 3-1. ANALYTICS MATURITY MODEL

STAGE	DESCRIPTION
1. Analytically Impaired	"Flying blind" – Lacks data, analysts, and executive interest
2. Localized Analytics	Pockets of analytical activity, but no coordinated activity or strategy
3. Analytical Aspirations	A few strategic initiatives underway but progress is slow
4. Analytical Companies	Benefits from regular use of analytics, but it's not strategic
5. Analytical Competitors	Widespread use of analytics which delivers a competitive advantage

From **Davenport, Tom, Jeanne Harris, and Robert Morison,** *Analytics at Work: Smarter Decisions, Better Results,* **Harvard Business Press, 2010, pp. 21-22.**

Fortunately, the analytical leaders profiled in this book have discovered the keys to analytical success. From a technical perspective, their recommendations seem straightforward: govern and curate the data; develop reports and dashboards that enable business users to monitor and manage critical processes; empower business analysts and statisticians to explore data and create models; and embed models into core operational applications and processes that run the business.

But the biggest factor that determines analytical success does not involve technology; rather, it involves leadership. Successful analytical leaders provide vision, guidance, and support to their teams, and they model and continually reinforce the importance of communication, teamwork, and execution. Specifically, they establish strong partnerships with top executives and business unit heads; they hire top-notch developers and analysts who understand the business and generate valuable insights; they organize and motivate their teams to deliver outstanding results; and they run projects that exceed user expectations and finish on time and within budget. In short, analytical leaders create and maintain a culture of excellence.

SELF ASSESSMENT

Using the lessons learned from analytical leaders profiled in this book, I created an analytical maturity model that provides an easy way to assess an organization's analytical IQ. (See Figure 3-2.) The quadrant chart plots four major dimensions of analytical IQ: data maturity, analytical maturity, analytical culture, and scale and scope. The business value of analytics increases as companies move from the lower left quadrant to the upper right one.

The top right quadrant consists of companies with high analytical and data maturity who are "analytical competitors." These companies treat analytics as a strategic enterprise resource and reap significant business value from their analytical initiatives. In contrast, the bottom left quadrant consists of companies with low analytical and data maturity that are "flying blind" because users lack access to trustworthy and consistent data and reports. Companies in these two quadrants are at polar ends of the maturity scale.

Companies in the remaining two quadrants are in the middling zone. The bottom right quadrant consists of companies with "analytical potential" that have done the hard work of creating a unified data infrastructure, but lack executive vision and analytical skills. The top left quadrant consists of companies that have "pockets of analytics" in departments and business units run by visionary executives, but lack an overall vision for analytics and an equivalent analytical infrastructure.

Analytical Maturity. Analytical maturity (left-hand axis) reflects the spectrum of analytical capabilities, from standard reporting to predictive analytics, that was depicted in Chapter 2. (See Figure 2-1, "Waves of Reporting and Analysis.") The lower half of the axis represents basic reporting and analysis skills, while the top half represents more advanced reporting and analysis capabilities. Some argue that dashboards should be in the lower half of the axis, but I disagree. It takes a great deal of analytical sophistication to create a layered MAD dashboard that displays core metrics tailored by role with three-click access to any data. (See Figure 2-3 "The MAD Dashboard Framework.")

FIGURE 3-2. ASSESSING YOUR ANALYTICAL IQ

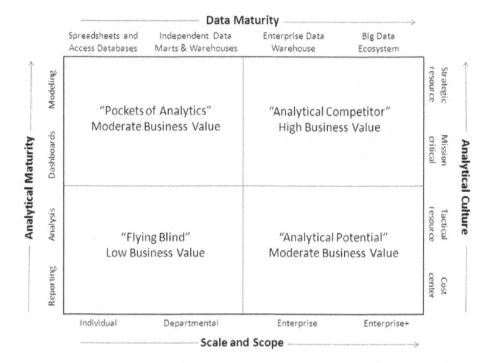

This analytical maturity model has four dimensions of analytical maturity. The quadrant chart makes it easy for organizations to track their maturity over time and compare the health of their analytical programs to those at other organizations.

Data Maturity. Data maturity (top horizontal axis) is the toughest dimension to master because it requires a sustained, coordinated effort by business and IT to deliver clean, consistent data on an enterprise scale. Executives from every business unit and department must agree to a single set of definitions for shared business terms and metrics. They must also fund a scalable infrastructure that integrates data from across the enterprise so that data is easily accessed and queried for decision-making purposes. Although CEOs can hire individuals to build reports, dashboards, and statistical models, they can't create a unified data infrastructure without buy-in from other executives and sustained funding over many years.

Five years ago, the Holy Grail for data management was an

enterprise data warehouse that consolidates shared data, either physically or virtually, into a single environment designed explicitly to support reporting and analysis applications. Today, the enterprise data warehouse is one of several critical pieces of infrastructure within an analytical ecosystem that supports reporting and analysis applications. New entrants into the analytical ecosystem include Hadoop, master data management, analytical sandboxes, and in-memory visualization applications. (See Chapter 17 for more details.)

Analytical Culture. As mentioned above, culture (right-hand axis) plays a major role in the success of analytical initiatives. Culture defines what things an organization does and how they do it. Executives set the tone by defining the vision, values, and strategy, while teams and individuals execute the strategy. Companies that compete on analytics have executives who view analytics as a strategic asset and mission-critical resource that drives core processes. Executives without such vision view analytics as a set of tactical tools to improve decision making, or worse, a cost-center that offers minimal return on investment.

Scale and Scope. Finally, the scale and scope of an analytical initiative (bottom-horizontal axis) increases with analytical IQ. Although it's easy to implement analytics in pockets throughout an organization, it is challenging to deliver analytics in a coordinated fashion throughout an enterprise. At most companies, analytics starts out as an individual effort by a SQL-savvy business analyst who creates just-in-time reports for busy executives and everyone else. In the next stage, executives fund data marts to support departmental applications. In the third stage, executives often backfill an enterprise data warehouse behind multiple data marts to eliminate informational turf wars, achieve economies of scale, and deliver a consistent view of enterprise data. In the final stage, organizations deploy analytics outside corporate firewalls to customers, suppliers, and prospects either as a value-added service or a commercial product, transforming analytics from a cost-center to a profit-center.

COMMENTARY FROM ANALYTICAL LEADERS

COLSON: Among the companies where I've worked, Netflix is the most data-driven. Its algorithms give it a competitive advantage. They enable Netflix to identify great television shows and movies for its content library and delight customers with personalized recommendations. Netflix makes decisions empirically through an experimentation framework. In fact, empiricism and science are part of Netflix's DNA and supported by its culture. Analytics is a massive muscle that Netflix has developed, and one that is hard for competitors to replicate.

In an analytical culture, business people avoid expressing opinions or pushing unsubstantiated ideas. Instead, they propose *hypotheses*, which they submit to testing and experimentation. They've been given training in basic statistical methods, so they know how to interpret the results of A/B tests, read p-values and significance levels, and assess false positives. They test every product feature before it rolls out and let the results of scientific experiments decide a new feature's fate, not politics or opinion.

Netflix is certainly a leader when it comes to applying data and analytics to business issues. And, like any industry leader intent on continuous improvement, they have ambitious plans to take things to the next level.

THEARLING: As an analytical consultant, I think the telltale sign of analytical maturity is when data flows smoothly through an organization like oil through a refinery. Ideally, data first flows to business analysts who identify new market opportunities, then to data analysts who validate those ideas, and then to statisticians who create analytical models that operationalize processes, and finally to operations managers who deliver the products.

To succeed with analytics, data must flow continuously, not on a periodic or one-off basis. Otherwise, the scramble to acquire data and feed it to operational processes contorts the business. Data-driven organizations are well-oiled machines when it comes to managing the flow of data that drives core processes.

LEONARD: I'd say U.S. Xpress is about a three on a five-point scale. During the past three years, we accomplished a lot with the help of the business. We implemented near real-time data feeds using telemetry data from our trucks, deployed a publish-and-subscribe messaging bus to interconnect our applications, deployed critical information via mobile devices, implemented Hadoop as a staging area for structured and unstructured data, standardized information about customers, drivers, trucks, and other reference data, and established a Business Intelligence (BI) Competency Center with strong executive participation. However, there is still a lot of work to do. U.S. Xpress needs to make it even easier for power users to create cubes without having to write SQL. And it needs to adopt analytical modeling in more of our departments that need it, among other things.

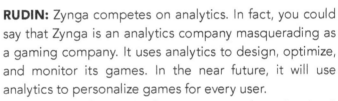

RUDIN: Zynga competes on analytics. In fact, you could say that Zynga is an analytics company masquerading as a gaming company. It uses analytics to design, optimize, and monitor its games. In the near future, it will use analytics to personalize games for every user.

For example, some of Zynga's games have "quests," which are a series of things players do to earn a prize or reward. Currently, every player in the game gets the same quest, which isn't ideal. Someone who plays the game only once or twice a week might find that the quest takes too long, and they get discouraged and quit. On the other hand, frequent players might find the quest too easy, so they get bored and quit. In either case, we aren't optimizing player engagement.

But with analytics, Zynga can create a custom quest for each player based on his or her playing habits and social network. For instance, the occasional player might need to collect five things, perform three tasks, and participate in one activity with five neighbors, while a frequent player might have to do twice as many things to complete the quest. Analytics enables Zynga to customize the game for each player to maximize their enjoyment and the amount of time they play.

INGLE: Kelley Blue Book has a high analytics IQ, but it's hard to know where the rest of the world stands. Culturally, we have embraced the strategic value of analytics. The company's growth depends on our ability to monetize data using analytics. We are sitting on an oil field of data, especially now that we're part of the AutoTrader Group, which includes AutoTrader.com, a large online publisher of classified vehicle listings that is nearly ten times larger than Kelley Blue Book. In the near future, we plan to sink a pipe below the surface of the combined companies and access all the data down there.

On the data side, we are relatively mature, although we always strive to accelerate our ability to ingest new data sources and make them available for analytics. To do that, we are building a more flexible framework for acquiring data. For example, instead of specifying every attribute of some source data, we would like to suck in all that data first, and then explore it before we model and load it into our data warehouse.

On the analytics side, we have created a partnership between statisticians and analysts to create our vehicle values. The statisticians use modeling techniques to create forecasts, and our analysts validate or refine those models based on their industry knowledge and experience. By blending art and science, this hybrid approach works well.

O'CONNOR: On one hand, we are mature on every axis of Wayne's maturity model. We are led by visionary executives who have placed smart data at the core of our strategy. We've deployed a big data ecosystem that collects and integrates data from a wide variety of sources that enable us to model how people interact with the physical world. We have a central team that manages our data asset. We have experts throughout the business to deliver subject matter analytical solutions. We've proven that we can use analytics to deliver better maps, routes, and consumer experiences.

On the other hand, we are still in the early phases of our journey to leverage big data. Although we have terabytes of activity data flowing around the world on a daily basis, we still have a mountain of work to do. For instance, we have to fine tune our applications and sensors to generate better data, and then clean the data we ingest. We also have to build more analytical models and further develop business practices that leverage smart data.

At a global organization like Nokia, it takes time to execute a new vision. The bottom line is that our appetite for analytics is huge, and we'll be cooking for a long time to satisfy it.

TAYLOR: Blue KC is currently about a 7 on a 10 point scale. Of course, on my scale, you never get to a 10 because the target always moves. We've definitely come a long way. Everyone now understands the importance of analytics, and we've invested substantially to build the right foundation for a best-in-class analytics program. Our biggest area of opportunities are retooling our report request culture, more fully exploiting what we've built, and increasing user adoption.

A top priority for us is to gain traction for self-service BI. We want to get individuals to start using our drillable dashboards instead of asking business analysts to build custom reports for them. One way that we're reducing report dependency is to deploy dashboards on tablet computers. Even though we've built equivalent Web and desktop applications, executives perceive that tablet-based applications are easier to use, so they are more willing to experiment and use the functionality.

Another way we've boosted self service is to give new BI tools to casual users before power users. This way, casual users are more apt to learn to use the new tools since they can't lean on power users to create custom reports for them. This helps break the cycle of report dependency and frees power users to do other work.

Blue KC is now hiring more sophisticated analysts (i.e., statisticians) because it finally has a data and analytics environment that can support their work. In the past, our analysts spent 80% of their time collecting and integrating data, rather than analyzing it. As a result, we couldn't retain them for long. So, we ended up outsourcing much of our advanced analytical work. But now we're ready to move to the next level and bring this competency in house.

SUMMARY

There are many assessments to gauge an organization's analytical IQ or maturity. The analytical maturity model discussed in this chapter places a premium on analytical culture, data infrastructure, analytical competency, and scale and scope. Although there are more factors involved in succeeding with analytics, an organization that scores well on these four dimensions has a strong chance of becoming an analytical competitor like those profiled in this book.

With a high analytical IQ, an organization is well positioned to deliver both bottom-line cost savings and strategic value through analytics, as our analytical leaders attest in the next chapter.

CHAPTER 4

WHAT IS THE VALUE OF ANALYTICS?

It's hard to put a dollar figure on the value of analytics. That is the general consensus of the analytical leaders profiled in this book. Most say that the biggest value of analytics is intangible. For instance, how do you calculate the impact of better decisions? Or, the value of integrated data? Or, deeper insights into customer behavior?

However, the analytical leaders uniformly say that analytics is a requirement for doing business and a strategic asset that provides a competitive advantage. Their organizations use analytics to improve products, optimize processes, monitor performance, maintain strong partnerships, and respond quickly to change, among other things.

For example, Ken Rudin shows how Zynga uses analytics to create more engaging games that customers want to play longer. Darren Taylor explains how analytics improves medical outcomes for Blue KC's members. Tim Leonard shows how analytics gives fleet managers at U.S. Xpress near real-time views of orders, trucks, and drivers so they can optimize shipments and revenues. And Amy O'Connor explains how Nokia is using analytics to create new data-driven products and services for mobile consumers and advertisers.

Tangible Benefits. Besides strategic advantages, analytics can provide tangible, bottom-line benefits, especially in the early stages of an analytics program. Here, companies can achieve economies of scale by consolidating duplicate reports and systems while dramatically increasing analyst productivity. For instance, Blue KC consolidated six independent analytical applications running in different departments, justifying the expense of implementing a new analytical infrastructure. In terms of worker productivity, an analytical manager at a large hardware manufacturer estimated that a new analytical infrastructure saved his company $10 million a year since analysts no longer had to spend several days each week hunting for data, integrating data sets, and formatting results.

DIMENSIONS OF VALUE

From Reactive to Proactive. One way to understand the value of analytics is to examine its primary dimensions. (See Figure 4-1.) Generally, the value of analytics increases as its focus shifts from the past to the present to the future. In other words, analytical applications that enable companies to work more proactively generally provide greater value.

FIGURE 4-1. THE VALUE OF ANALYTICS

Category	Time	Purpose	Tools	Users	Value
Reporting	Past	View the past	Operational reports, ad hoc reports, enterprise reports	Casual users	Moderate
Analysis	Past	Explain the past	Excel, ad hoc query, OLAP, visual discovery	Business analysts	Moderate
Monitoring	Present	Monitor the present	Dashboards, scorecards	Casual users	Moderate/High
Prediction	Present/Future	Optimize the present or predict the future	Statistical models, machine learning, and optimization	Statisticians, operations researchers	High
Hypothesis testing	Present/Future	Test assumptions and evaluate scenarios	A/B testing, "what if" models, planning models, simulation	Business analysts, statisticians	High

For instance, reporting, analysis, and monitoring to some extent look at the business from a rear view mirror. They enable business people to analyze historical activity. Here, insights lead to actions after the fact. Nonetheless, there is still significant value in such analytical activity. For instance, reports lead to better plans, and analyses help answer critical ad hoc questions, such as "Why did sales drop yesterday?" or "How much did customers who purchased three or more distinct products spend with us last month?" Operational dashboards, on the other hand, monitor business activity in near-real time, enabling business people to act while the business activity is still happening and before its impact appears on the bottom line.

Predictive applications offer even higher value since they help companies anticipate the future and work proactively instead of reactively. For instance, an organization with hundreds of field technicians might use an analytical model to optimize schedules and routes, minimizing travel time and fuel costs. Finally, hypothesis-driven testing delivers significant value because it enables users to evaluate their assumptions with scientific precision. For example, internet companies might use A/B testing to evaluate whether new Web features offer sufficient revenue lift before rolling them out. And financial services firms might use what-if modeling and simulation techniques (e.g., Monte Carlo methods) to select the best investments based on many different market scenarios.

Strategic to Operational. Another way to assess the value of analytics is by types of decisions. (See Figure 4-2.) In the past, organizations used analytical tools to make *strategic* decisions, such as whether to introduce a new product line, acquire a competitor, change a pricing model, or expand the sales force. These types of decisions are few in number, but significant in impact.

FIGURE 4-2. THE IMPACT OF DIFFERENT TYPES OF DECISIONS

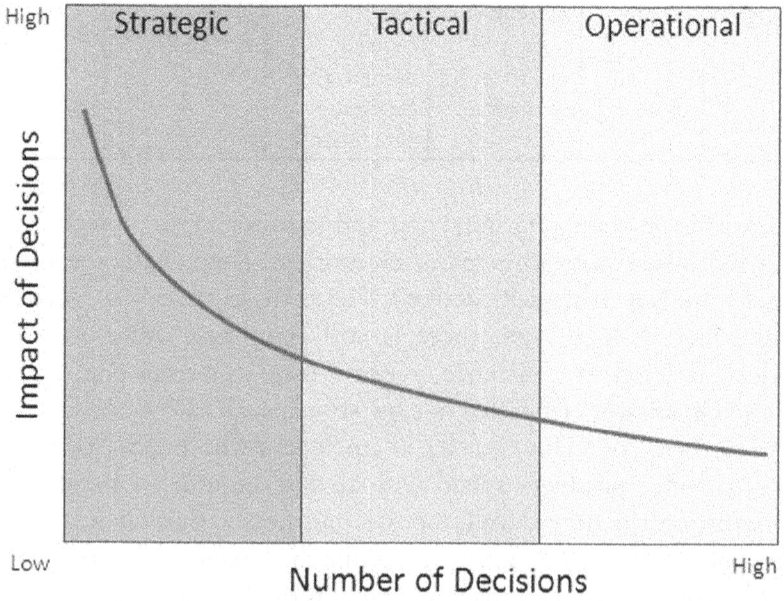

This chart shows the relationship between business impact and volume for three types of decisions.

In contrast, a growing number of organizations use analytics to make *operational* decisions, such as deciding how best to route a truck to accommodate a new order, accommodate passengers on a late arriving flight, or replace a defective part on a production line. These decisions are many in number but smaller in impact. Somewhere in between are *tactical* decisions, which enable departmental managers and staff to optimize processes, such as how to allocate budgeted resources, craft a new marketing promotion, or analyze the impact of a new system or project.

Applying analytics to different types of decisions delivers different degrees of value. On the whole, each type of decision delivers equivalent value if you multiply the number of instances by their impact.

ANALYTICAL APPLICATIONS

Finally, analytics is an equal opportunity provider. Every industry and functional area—from marketing and sales to procurement and finance—can reap the benefits of data-driven reporting and analysis applications, including advanced analytics.

When it comes to advanced analytics, marketing is the biggest departmental user. (See Figure 4-3.) It uses statistical models to identify cross-sell and upsell opportunities, optimize campaigns and promotions, target the right customers for each offer, and reduce churn. Finance and sales use analytics to forecast revenues, while operations managers use it to identify fraud.

Additionally, every industry profits from advanced analytics, especially those with large numbers of customers, partners, suppliers, parts, or products—and that's most large companies today. (See Figure 4-4.) In many industries, the information about products and customers is just as important as the products themselves. This is certainly true for information-rich industries, such as banking, insurance, healthcare, telecommunications, government, internet, and media. For example, Kelley Blue Book considers itself as much of an analytics company as a publisher since it now uses analytics to calculate car valuations.

**FIGURE 4-3. FUNCTIONAL APPLICATIONS OF
ADVANCED ANALYTICS**

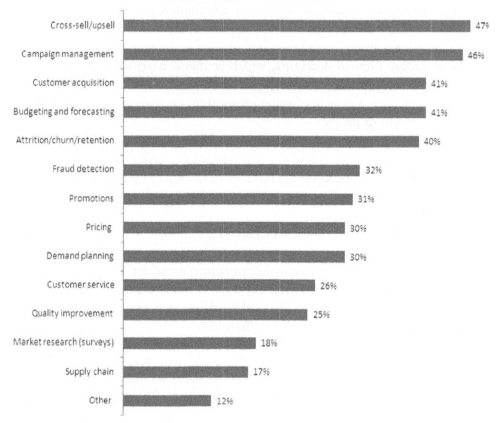

From Wayne Eckerson, "Predictive Analytics: Extending the Value of Your Data Warehousing Investments," The Data Warehousing Institute, 2007.

There are numerous ways to reap value from an analytics program. Early on, analytics can deliver significant cost savings by consolidating redundant reporting systems. Later on, it can drive core processes, providing organizations with a strategic advantage in the marketplace.

FIGURE 4-4. ANALYTICAL APPLICATIONS BY INDUSTRY

Retail	Pricing and merchandising optimization, promotions analysis, demand forecasting, inventory replenishment, shelf management, sentiment analysis
Manufacturing	Supply chain optimization, demand forecasting, inventory replenishment, warranty analysis, product customization, product development
Banking	Credit scoring, fraud detection, pricing optimization, customer profitability, risk management, loan underwriting, cross-sell and upsell promotions, customer churn
Insurance	Fraud detection, claims analysis, contract pricing, agency management, customized pricing based on activity
Transportation	Scheduling, routing, yield management, maintenance optimization, logistics, fuel usage, load management, driver performance
Healthcare	Disease management, drug interactions, preventive care, physician performance, contract management, throughput and wait times, cost management
Energy	Platform and pipeline maintenance, trading analysis, seismic analysis, forecasting, compliance controls and analysis
Government	Fraud detection, case management, crime prevention, spatial analysis, economic forecasting, case management
Internet	Customer retention, churn analysis, customer interaction, social network analysis, recommendation engines, sentiment analysis
Communications	Traffic analysis, network utilization, social graphs, location intelligence, target marketing and promotions, sentiment analysis

Adapted from "Analytics at Work" by Tom Davenport, Jeanne Harris, and Robert Morison (Wiley 2010).

COMMENTARY FROM ANALYTICAL LEADERS

INGLE: It's hard to put a dollar figure on the value of analytics at Kelley Blue Book. Publishing values for new and used cars is the core of what we do and the foundation of our brand. We use analytics to generate those values, so how do you calculate the value or ROI of that?

Analytics has changed the DNA of Kelley Blue Book and the way it works. Analytics has enabled us to significantly improve the effectiveness of our vehicle values, while dramatically expanding the number of values we produce without adding any analysts. We now publish weekly values for more than 20,000 cars and trucks with hundreds of combinations of vehicle options across 51 regions in the U.S. That's about a 15-fold increase from several years ago when we published monthly values across a handful of regions using a more manual process. This has been a huge win.

When I arrived at Kelley Blue Book six years ago, the company created vehicle valuations with some science and a lot of intuition rooted in deep industry experience. Given rapid advances in technology and data accessibility and the volatility in the automotive market, we had to embrace a more analytically driven approach to creating vehicle values or we would have struggled to remain relevant in a fast-paced market.

WEB ANALYTICS. We also use analytics to optimize the advertising on our Web site. Today, we can forecast Web traffic for a year in advance to within a few percentage points, which helps us determine our advertising inventory and capacities section by section on the Web site. For example, we are penalized if we don't deliver a guaranteed number of ad impressions for a specific buy, but we lose if we over-deliver on impressions since those overages are not monetized. So, analytics helps us walk this fine line.

RUDIN: The online gaming industry used to fly blind, analytically speaking. It was all about getting creative people to design games and hope that people liked and played them. It was very much like the movie industry where you hire great writers, actors, and producers, hope they dream up something magical, and then publish it to the world.

But Zynga's CEO, Mark Pincus, invented a new analytics-driven approach that has revolutionized how the multi-billion dollar gaming industry works. Today, Zynga's game designers receive constant analytical feedback about how people interact with their games that they incorporate into subsequent designs. Thus, today's online games are more like a situation comedy series on television than a movie. In a situation comedy, writers change the plot or characters based on audience feedback. In the same way, Zynga tracks player behavior and adjusts the games to make them more interesting and enjoyable as well as meet its goals for retention and revenue.

ANALYTICS USE CASES. Specifically, Zynga uses analytics to do three things: 1) monitor the health of its games in real time, 2) help design the games, and 3) personalize a game player's experience.

In terms of monitoring, Zynga scans its game data in real time to look for abnormal patterns. For instance, it might see one critical metric—such as daily active users—decrease after the release of a new version of a game. So, Zynga will immediately roll back to the prior version of the game and then figure out what happened.

Zynga also uses analytics to help design its games. It instruments games to capture all kinds of information about how a person interacts with the game—what they did, how long they stayed, how frequently they return, and so on. For instance, a single player's session might generate a thousand data points that are deposited in Zynga's data warehouse within a few minutes and analyzed for ways to improve the games. Interestingly, when Zynga launches a new game, the designers only create enough content to engage a player for the first few weeks. After that, they look at the analytics to determine what game features to add or modify.

Finally, Zynga is beginning to use analytics to personalize the game experience. For instance, a game might recommend to a player other people who might want to play a game with them based on their playing profile. Rather than inviting them to play with their Facebook friends, like Zynga does now, it can make more astute recommendations and find more ideal gaming partners based on how people actually play the game.

LEONARD: Analytics has the power to reshape the business landscape. In our case, one of the applications we built enabled U.S. Xpress to restructure its core operational processes, a strategic move that made the company more agile and competitive, and saved money.

Our fleet managers used to share a pool of customer service representatives and planners, but this led to conflict and finger pointing. Our new XPM fleet management application puts all relevant information at the fingertips of every fleet manager. XPM is a Web-based application that replaced an AS/400 system with hundreds of green screens. The application, which runs on our real-time data warehouse, delivers all relevant information in a few screens, giving fleet managers a real-time view of every aspect of their operations, from drivers to trucks to orders to alerts.

For example, if fleet managers want to know about a driver, they can click on his name and see his background, driving history, ratings, days on the road, and distance from home, all of which get factored into dispatch calls. The system also lets fleet managers view the location and status of each truck on a map, as well as its maintenance record, destination, current carrying capacities, and order queue. In essence, the application makes it easier for fleet managers to route orders, dispatch trucks, and optimize carrying capacity, which makes our shipping services more competitive and efficient.

The application also funnels alerts to fleet managers in near real-time so they can react quickly to new conditions on the road. For instance, if a driver is delayed by traffic, an alert will notify a fleet manager, who can reroute other trucks to pick up the load. The system blends operational and analytical capabilities. Essentially, it embeds business intelligence (BI) and data warehousing data into a mission critical operational application that is much simpler to learn and use than the old system. It used to take months for fleet managers to learn how to use the AS/400 system; now it takes days to learn XPM.

With XPM in place, our executive team restructured the company into autonomous, regional fleets or "pods", each of which now have their own customer service representatives and planners. Our CEO, Max Fuller, told me, "Without XPM and your new data architecture, we wouldn't have been able to restructure our operations, which is something we've wanted to do for a very long time."

TAYLOR: Blue KC has delivered a lot of tangible and intangible value from both our data warehouse and analytical environment.

Our data warehouse integrates data from about 75 source systems throughout the organization and it feeds about 20 different transaction systems, including the general ledger, care management system, and actuarial and underwriting systems, to name a few. We've saved considerable time by giving our developers one place to go to get all the data they need to run analyses or feed applications. As a result, we've accelerated time to market for many new applications. It's hard to put a dollar figure on this, but the data warehouse is a valuable asset for Blue KC.

In terms of analytics, we're reducing our overhead by consolidating six analytical applications into a single system and standardizing data definitions and rules. We have already eliminated about $3 million in annual software licensing and associated infrastructure costs, and our new platform will pay for itself in 2.5 years. And we've turned our analytical infrastructure and applications into a commercial offering that will generate revenues and profits for the company.

FROM REACTIVE TO PROACTIVE. However, the real value of our analytics initiative is difficult to quantify. Analytics helps us move from a reactive to proactive approach to addressing business problems and opportunities. Previously, if our top-level metrics showed a significant negative variance, we would run around like crazy trying to figure out the problem and who was accountable. Today, our analytical environment enables us to systematically analyze our key metrics at a deeper level. For instance, by understanding what drives medical costs, we have identified several opportunities to reduce those costs by about 5%.

For example, we discovered an opportunity to reduce the number of costly and ineffective elective surgeries, especially back surgeries, through educational programs. We also identified potential cost savings by coordinating physicians who care for members with multiple chronic conditions (e.g., diabetes and heart disease) as well as restructuring some provider contracts to better fit changing conditions.

The point is that instead of waiting for a crisis, we now do a much better job of using data to identify problems and opportunities in advance and work proactively to address them. We're shifting staff from low-value activities to

high-value initiatives. We still have a lot of work to do to achieve all the opportunities we've identified and improve medical outcomes for members, but
analytics has enabled us to move in the right direction.

O'CONNOR: Analytics is a top-level strategic initiative
at Nokia. And that's because we're using analytics across
a spectrum of value propositions. We use analytics to
drive business transparency, which often results in greater
efficiencies and lower costs. For example, we use it optimize
our supply chain.

We also use data and analytics to improve our products.
For instance, we are replacing manual methods of updating maps with automated
methods based on big data analytics. Today, Nokia phones generate ten billion
probes monthly, which are anonymized data points that show the direction and
speed of the device at a given point in time. With enough data points, we
can determine whether the actual flow of people matches our maps or not.
For instance, the data might indicate a two-way road instead of the one-way
road depicted on our map. Using analytical models on this probe data, we can
automatically correct maps to reflect what is going on in the real world.

But Nokia is also using analytics to create a new generation of data-
driven products. Besides activity data from sensors in phones, we have data
on 18 million miles of roads, accident reports from 24 countries, public transit
schedules, and 80 million points of interest, including businesses and schools,
among other things. As a result, many consumer businesses use our location
services, including Bing, Yahoo, Garmin, Foursquare, and Yelp. So we gather a
lot of activity and location data from these applications. We are now using all
this data to index the real world. We want to make it as easy to navigate the real
world as it is to navigate the Web. That's our goal for analytics at Nokia.

COLSON: Data and analytics are like oxygen to internet
companies. They don't just provide a competitive advantage;
they help run the businesses. For example, analytics is
how Netflix decides which television shows and movies to
recommend to customers and which features to add to its
products and Web sites. Analytics and data are so fundamental to internet companies that these companies don't debate their value
because they couldn't survive a day without them. I suspect that many other

industries value data and analytics in the same way, but I'm most familiar with internet companies.

Most internet companies today capture terabytes of data a day that describe what customers do on their Web sites: what page objects they look at, what ads they click on, what sites they came from and depart for, and so on. They gather all the information about what customers do before and after they make transactions so they can better understand what drives their purchases. Before the Web, you couldn't gather this type of behavioral data; and without analytics, you couldn't study this behavior in detail. So, data warehousing and analytics are business critical assets that help companies deliver better products and services and differentiate themselves in the marketplace.

SUMMARY

The value of analytics is simple: it helps organizations make smarter decisions, improve performance, and achieve strategic objectives. It moves organizations from reacting to situations and fighting fires to proactively addressing issues and opportunities. Analytics, when first deployed, can often reduce costs by eliminating redundant overhead and increasing worker productivity. But the real value of analytics comes when organizations apply it strategically to improve their products, processes, partnerships, and customer relationships.

Of course, you can't reap the value from analytics if you don't execute properly. In the next chapter, our analytical leaders summarize their secrets to running a successful analytical program.

CHAPTER 5

WHAT ARE THE KEYS TO ANALYTICAL SUCCESS?

The analytical leaders profiled in this book describe many keys to success. This chapter summarizes their keys to running an effective analytics program, while subsequent chapters dive into greater detail on the themes and subjects highlighted here.

Ironically, the analytical leaders spend as much time discussing how to manage people, projects, and processes as they do technology and architectures, which they view as enablers. Specifically, Tim Leonard emphasizes the need to understand the business and talk its language, while Dan Ingle focuses on building applications quickly through agile development approaches. Others, including Darren Taylor and Amy O'Connor, underscore the importance of obtaining strong executive sponsorship, while Kurt Thearling and others emphasize the need of getting a quick win to establish credibility and momentum for an analytics program. And every analytical leader emphasizes the importance of curating data and moving beyond insights to action.

Change management. Analytics requires both strong analytical leaders and executives who are willing to make a long-term commitment to its success. Analytics is not a one-time project; it's a program—or as some say, a journey that requires a long-term investment of time, money, and expertise. It requires organizations to treat data as a corporate asset and invest in building an analytical infrastructure. Moreover, it requires workers to change the way they view and manage data, and frame and make decisions. This involves changing core processes as well as modifying individual and group habits, which is hard to do. Ultimately, as Amy O'Connor emphasizes, analytics is an exercise in change management.

STEPS TO SUCCESS

To succeed with analytics, organizations need the right culture, people, organization, architecture, and data. (See Figure 5-1.) This is a tall order. Putting these pieces in place involves more than just technical expertise; it requires an organizational overhaul that has to start at the top and ripple through the rest of the organization. There is as much "soft" stuff involved in succeeding with analytics as "hard" stuff. That's why most of the analytical leaders profiled in this book spend much time discussing selling, marketing, and teamwork as they spend talking about technology and tools.

The Right Culture. Culture refers to the rules—both written and unwritten—for how things get done in an organization. These rules emanate primarily from the words and actions of top executives. Business executives must have a vision for analytics and the willingness to invest in the people, processes, and technologies for the long haul to ensure a successful outcome (See Chapter 6). Technical executives must be able to talk the language of business and recruit business people to work on their teams. They also need to manage all components of the analytics program, from data warehousing to business intelligence to advanced analytics.

The Right People. It's impossible to do analytics without data developers and analysts. Data developers build and maintain the data structures (e.g., data warehouse, data marts, master data management, BI semantic layers) and create complex reports and dashboards. Analysts, on the other hand, explore the data and generate reports and dashboards to answer ad hoc questions asked by the business. Hiring and retaining the right people is not easy. Both data developers and analysts require a passion for data, along with a blend of people skills, technical expertise, and business knowledge (See Chapter 8).

The Right Organization. Every company needs to cultivate a federated organizational model to succeed with analytics. Centrally, it needs a center of excellence that establishes and inculcates best practices for building analytical applications and provides a forum for team members to share ideas and techniques. Departmentally, it needs embedded data developers who can quickly build data-driven solutions as well as embedded analysts who can quickly address ad hoc questions. Sometimes, these are one and the same person, but not always. In addition, a federated organization needs to manage shared data as an enterprise resource while empowering departments to build their own reports, dashboards, and analytical models. This dual focus requires some tricky organizational choreography that most companies have yet to master. (See Chapter 9.)

FIGURE 5-1. ANALYTICAL FRAMEWORK

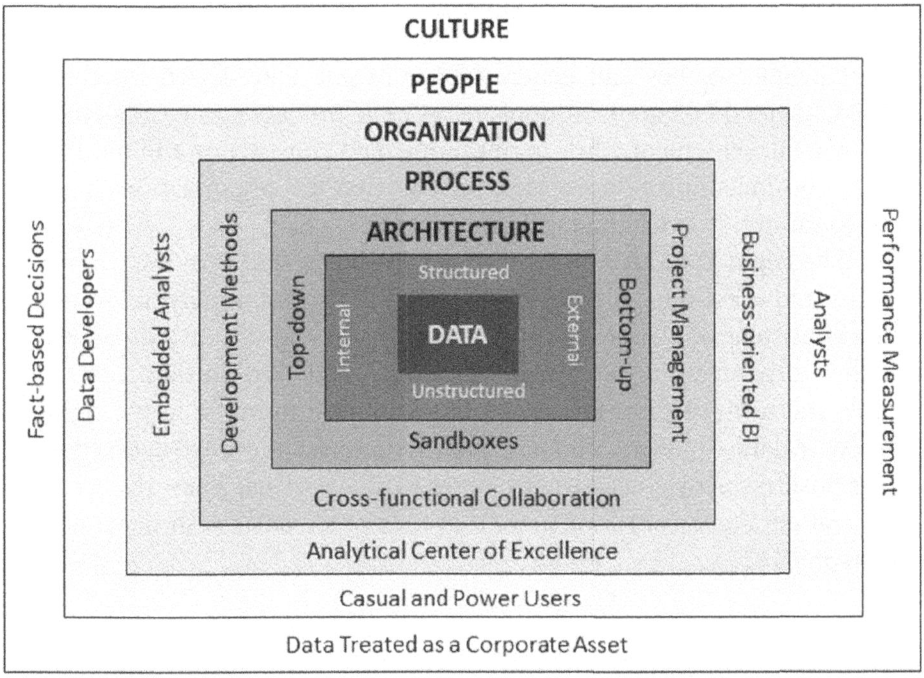

This framework highlights the major areas required to run a successful analytics program.

The Right Process. A hallmark of an outstanding analytical program is that it has standard processes and procedures for doing things, such as managing projects, developing software, gathering requirements, communicating across business functions, deploying analytical models, handling job errors, designing and changing data models, evaluating and selecting new tools and technologies, and ingesting external data, among other things. However, analytical managers must be careful not to overburden their teams with too many processes and standards that impede agility and undermine flexibility, as Eric Colson cautions later in this chapter. Part II of this book deals with various analytical processes: managing people (Chapter 10), developing software (Chapter 11), delivering insights and action (Chapter 12), and developing analytical models (Chapter 13).

The Right Architecture. Every analytical organization needs tools and technologies to do its work. The ideal architecture creates a data assembly line in which data flows from sources to targets to applications, each tailored to different departments and types of users. It extends existing data warehousing environments with new database processing platforms and complements top-down monitoring with bottom-up ad hoc exploration. It also provides the right tools to the right people so they can generate or consume data-driven insights. (See Chapter 17). Finally, it implements agile processes that accelerate software development while maintaining data consistency and models across business units—a sizable challenge that few organizations have yet to master. (See Chapters 11 and 15.)

The Right Data. Analytics also requires data that is in the proper shape and condition. It must be complete, accurate, timely, relevant, and consistent or business people won't trust it and stop using it, even if their organization has invested millions of dollars in data-centric tools and technologies. Organizations also need to invest in the right kinds of data—internal and external, structured and unstructured—that business people need to answer critical questions. They also need to treat data as a corporate asset that is as precious as cash or people (Chapter 14).

COMMENTARY FROM ANALYTICAL LEADERS

RUDIN: You succeed with analytics when you stay focused on the end goal. It isn't enough to find patterns in the data and highlight trends and outliers in fancy charts, or deliver insights that can potentially drive business value. Your analysts must actually *create* business value. If nothing changes because of their insights, then they haven't added any value to the business. They have to strive to get the business to implement their insights so that they ensure a positive business impact. That means they have to talk with business people and brainstorm ways to turn their insights into business value. The insights can impact the business in many ways. They can change product designs, pricing, or processes, among other things.

Just like a salesperson takes ownership of an account and doesn't get paid commission unless he makes a sale, it doesn't make sense to reward analysts for delivering insights that aren't implemented; you should reward them for delivering value. And you measure value just like everything else. The key is to focus on impacts not insights.

ASK THE RIGHT QUESTIONS. I also think it's more important to ask the right questions than to get the right answers. It's easy to get answers. We know how to do that, and we have a ton of technology to help in this area. What's hard is asking the right questions which are going to drive business impact. A lot of this is about surfacing and testing assumptions about what people think drives behavior or business metrics. For example, game design is very creative but is based on a lot of assumptions, like "We can make the game more enjoyable and get people to play longer if we add this feature or change how hard it is to get to the next level in the game." If you pose these assumptions as questions and test them, then you can prove them right or wrong. That's key to gaining understanding.

EMBED ANALYSTS. Finally, it's important to embed analysts inside the business teams they support. They need to sit side-by-side with business people, participate in all their meetings, and contribute their analytical knowledge and perspective. If they're not embedded, they can't possibly master the nuances of the business they're trying to support. It will take them much longer to perform an analysis and they might miss important details. Also, if they're not embedded, it's harder for them to persuade businesspeople to test their assumptions and act on the output to improve the business.

LEONARD: To succeed with analytics, you need to put as much emphasis on the "business" as on "intelligence." I rose up through the technical ranks and learned the hard way that you can't be perceived as an IT person. You need to be perceived as a business person who uses technology to solve business problems.

So my keys to success are: 1) talk the language of business, 2) let the business do the talking, and 3) get quick wins and build on your success. Ultimately, it's all about sales. It took me some time to check my technical content and language at the door to the executive suite. I discovered that the more I discussed architectures, schemas, and tools, the less business people seemed interested in what I had to say. But if I talked about business concerns, say increasing wafer counts per square foot of factory floor at a semiconductor company, then executives paid attention.

When I join a new company, I spend a lot of time listening to people and learning how the business works. If I open my mouth too soon and expose my business ignorance, I lose credibility. So, I try to master the business quickly. As I gain knowledge and confidence, I ask fewer questions and begin engaging in conversations. At some point, I know almost as much about the business as the business people. You know you've made it when a business person says, "You know a lot about the business for an IT guy!"

I also discovered that in key situations—like when you need executive support for a project—it's best to shut up and let the business people do the talking. While executives appreciate a business-savvy IT person, they would rather hear a business person explain the need for a business intelligence (BI) solution. So, when it's appropriate, I ask business people to deliver the presentations about data proposals, and I sit in the back and talk only if called upon.

To deliver successful projects, it's also critical to follow a clear methodology that involves plenty of dialogue between business and the BI team. Executives need to define objectives, communicate them to everyone involved, define measures of success, and hold someone accountable for the outcome. The development team needs to hire the right people, with appropriate technical and business skills, to develop the infrastructure and applications. The business needs to assign the right business people to work with the development team to define requirements and provide continual feedback to ensure applications meet their objectives and needs.

COLSON: The key to success starts with getting the right people. I've learned that it's far more important to hire people with the right personal qualities than the right technical skills. You want people who are curious, creative, tenacious, and passionate about what they do. People with those qualities quickly learn the technical skills they need, whether it's a new programming language, like Python, or a new analytical tool. They just do it. To them, technology is a means to an end.

It's important to pay for top talent. In a creative field like analytics, the best people perform ten times better than average people. It's much more effective to hire one "rock star" and pay him or her a big salary than hire several average performers. And, top performers want to work with other top performers, and this creates a virtuous cycle.

CULTURE. The right culture also matters. A data-driven culture that values empiricism keeps politics and opinions in check. People frame their ideas as hypotheses and submit them to testing and experimentation. Although decisions are evaluated scientifically, there is still room for judgment and intuition. This kind of culture values data and analytics immensely, creating a supportive environment in which data developers and analysts thrive. The right culture also minimizes rules and processes to prevent stifling innovation and learning. It continually prunes processes that don't add value and is willing to incur some risk to ensure a fluid, fast-moving environment.

ORGANIZATION. To get the most value from your people and culture, you need the right organizational structure. I prefer a federated organization in which a central team supports the activities of embedded data developers and analysts while giving them ample opportunities to collaborate and share knowledge. Here, data developers sit side by side with the business people they support. As a result, they become immersed in the business and more effective at what they do. In a federated organization, you align first with the business, and then optimize technical functions.

ROLES. In a dynamic business environment, data developers with a diversity of skills trump a collection of specialists. Specialization is a fine thing when you have well-defined requirements. But in a fast-moving company, developers need to *discover* requirements as they go. By developing an entire solution from requirements to testing, they can respond immediately, iterate rapidly, and deliver optimal solutions more quickly than a team of specialists that require endless meetings to coordinate their activities. The ideal data developer focuses on mastering a business domain rather than a technical specialty.

With the right people, culture, organization, and roles, you can create a high-performance analytical team.

 **INGLE:** My keys to success are pretty straightforward: 1) build things iteratively and incrementally using an agile development process, 2) adapt to circumstances and not be wedded to a particular solution or methodology, and 3) foster teamwork to increase productivity and effectiveness.

AGILE DEVELOPMENT. When I started in this space, I saw quite a few data warehousing projects blow up because they used a traditional development approach with an extended project timeline. To avoid that, I began applying rapid prototyping techniques. I'd quickly gather requirements for a subject area, deliver a working prototype in a few weeks, and make rapid adjustments, if needed. In essence, I was following the tenets of Scrum before the term came into vogue. Since then, I've adopted Scrum in a big way, adapting the methodology to data warehousing and business intelligence solutions. Typically, we use three-week sprints, storyboards, and small self-organizing teams to deliver working code based on user priorities. We also co-locate the developers and business users during the duration of the effort. It works really well and makes logical sense.

OPENNESS. Another key is to adapt your approach to the circumstances. I see a lot of people who are wed to a particular technology, vendor, or methodology because that's what they've known and made them successful. It's also easier and seemingly less risky to use something tried and true, rather than something new.

For instance, when I joined Kelley Blue Book, we were heavily vested in the Microsoft platform. We had many Microsoft products in house and plenty of people with Microsoft expertise. At the time, I couldn't imagine using a database other than Microsoft SQL Server, but we were also looking to scale up our environment to support much larger data volumes. One member of our team had experience with analytic appliances at a prior company, so we decided to evaluate several products. We trusted the findings of our proofs of concept, and ended up purchasing our first IBM Netezza appliance to power our data warehouse and other environments. That was one of the best decisions we made.

TEAMWORK. Finally, teamwork is essential to our success. We hold classes on teamwork and put our folks through various exercises—some of which are not for the fainthearted. The classes teach people how to communicate, ask questions when they don't understand something and open up to each other. Without a foundation of trust, a team can't work together effectively and its productivity suffers. Our focus on teamwork complements our agile approach to application development.

THEARLING: There are numerous things that organizations overlook when implementing advanced analytics. One is the importance of curating your data—that is, deciding what data to make available for analysis, and organizing that data so it's easy for users to find and access. This is not just data quality, which is also important, but for different reasons. Curating data is something a lot of organizations overlook or undervalue.

Another key success factor revolves around putting analytical models into production. It's critical for organizations to establish robust processes and build an automated infrastructure to manage predictive models in a cost-effective and compliant manner. This is especially true for companies that generate tens of millions of analytical scores a day, and whose models are subject to external regulations. These production-oriented processes are often necessary to comply with various regulations governing the use of consumer information and analytical models. And, when done right, they are also a source of competitive advantage.

TAYLOR: The three keys to creating a successful analytics program are: 1) obtain strong executive understanding and support, 2) deliver quick, meaningful business wins, and 3) make one person and group accountable for the program.

EXECUTIVE SUPPORT. We had great executive support when we built our data warehouse in 2004, and we quickly delivered good results. It took a bit longer to garner the same level of support for our analytical solution in 2010. Although our data warehousing program was alive and well, we distributed the delivery of analytical applications to individual departments with no single point of account-ability. It took us about 12 to 18 months to clarify the difference between data warehousing and analytics to our executive team and gain funding for a new analytical initiative. But once we received executive team support, we quickly implemented the analytical platform and then started reselling analytical services to other health plans.

DELIVER VALUE ALONG THE WAY. It's also important to deliver value along the way. You can't wait two years to produce something. For instance, while we were building our analytical infrastructure, we built two applications for executives to demonstrate the emerging value of the system. One was a financial dashboard for mobile devices that replaced a 76-page PDF document, and the other was an analysis of the federal subsidies that our members might receive under the new Affordable Care Act. These small, but valuable, business wins gave executives confidence that we would execute the analytical vision.

CLEAR AUTHORITY. Finally, it's important that one person heads the analytical initiative and is held accountable for its performance. We tried a matrix approach in which both IT and business departments manage the data warehousing program, but that didn't work. We later pulled the program out of IT and put it directly under the CIO, with the COO as the executive business sponsor and then handpicked staff to serve on the team. By knocking down some organizational walls and putting one person in charge with the right team members, we achieved much better results.

O'CONNOR: The way that we'll succeed at Nokia is to create a culture that treats data as our most critical asset. The keys to making this happen are executive support, evangelism, and collaboration. I don't have technology at the top of this list because that part comes easy to people at Nokia.

We have many smart, technical people at Nokia who have used open source tools to download data and create information silos. However, we have to stop creating these silos if we want to achieve our vision of 'smart data'. We have an executive leader who believes that 'smart data' is Nokia's differentiator going forward, and he makes it clear that data silos are no longer an acceptable way of doing business. The goal is a single, unified data asset.

Since executive mandates alone do not ensure successful change, we also need evangelism to ensure analytical success. Our key executive sponsor highlights 'smart data' stories at internal employee events, customer meetings, and industry keynotes. Internally, we document and publish these success stories to remind employees about the importance of analytical projects.

And the third key to our analytical success is collaboration. Although we have a centralized analytics group responsible for building the technology ecosystem and shared data asset, we rely on subject matter experts in each business group to develop analytical applications and services to drive our smart data initiative.

SUMMARY

There are many factors involved in running a successful analytics program. But providing the right culture, people, organization, architecture, and data are the basis for success. We'll examine the outer layers of the framework in Part II of this book—that's the "soft stuff" of people, projects, and processes.

PART II:
THE SOFT STUFF: MANAGING PEOPLE, PROJECTS, AND PROCESSES

CHAPTER 6

HOW DO YOU GAIN EXECUTIVE SUPPORT?

Two types. There are two types of business executives when it comes to analytics: enlightened and unenlightened. Enlightened executives instinctively understand the value of analytics and don't hesitate to make sizable investments in it. Unenlightened executives make you play the chicken-and-egg game: they won't invest in analytics until they see a return, but you can't show a return until they make an investment.

It's no secret that analytics programs grow and thrive under the leadership of enlightened executives. All the analytical leaders profiled in this book are fortunate enough to work for executives who recognize that running a data-driven organization is good for business. However, this doesn't mean that selling an analytics program to these executives is a cakewalk. As we'll see in this chapter and the next, a good analytical leader continuously evangelizes, markets, and sells the value of an analytics program to the executive team.

Tactical justification. When you begin an analytical journey, it's possible to justify investments through cost savings alone as we discussed in Chapter 4. That's because early-stage analytics programs typically have hundreds or thousands of spreadmarts, reporting systems, and other analytical silos that suck up precious time and resources. Consolidating these redundant systems into an enterprise analytical infrastructure eliminates overlap in people, processes, hardware, and software, and delivers cost-savings through economies of scale. Such consolidation efforts also frees up business analysts to spend more time analyzing data, rather than acting as pseudo data developers who source, clean, and integrate data for a living.

Strategic justification. Once an organization squeezes all the cost savings out of its analytical assembly line, then it needs to justify additional investment through strategic value alone. Successful analytical leaders establish a track record of delivering business value. They earn credibility project by project, delivering greater value with each new investment of time, money, and people. Once executives see that analytics supports mission-critical processes or deliver a competitive advantage, they often continue to invest in the technology, people, and processes. But one success doesn't guarantee continued support. Since executives come and go, successful analytical leaders must continually sell the benefits of analytics.

Approaches. The analytical leaders profiled in this book use various approaches to gain executive support. Darren Taylor, of Blue KC, put together a business plan to convince executives to invest in a new analytical data mart to supplement the company's data warehouse. Tim Leonard spent a lot of time learning the business so he could "talk the talk" of business and gain credibility as a business savvy technologist. Dan Ingle used his past data warehousing experiences to answer questions that Kelley Blue Book executives asked about how to compete on analytics. Amy O'Connor works for enlightened executives who want her to build a data asset that can help Nokia transform mountains of data into new digital products and services.

Ditch the dummy? Unfortunately, not every analytical leader is as lucky as those profiled in this book. I usually counsel people who work for unenlightened executives to be patient. Sometimes, these executives see the light and realize the importance of investing in analytics. At other times, they make one too many bad decisions based on gut feel or faulty data, and the board sends them packing. In either case, it's important to be ready when the opportunity arises to present a case for investing in analytics and a roadmap for development. Of course, if the status quo never changes, then at some point, you have to cut your losses and find a company that is more receptive to analytics and data-driven performance measurement. There is no use banging your head against the wall forever.

CHECKLIST FOR A NEW ANALYTICAL SPONSOR

What is the hallmark of an enlightened executive who makes a great analytical sponsor and helps get an analytics program off the ground? Here is a checklist that you can use when searching for an executive to sponsor an analytical initiative during the startup phase. (Once your analytics program takes root, then you need an executive steering committee that reviews the analytical roadmap, prioritizes initiatives, and secures funding. See Chapter 8.)

To establish a successful analytics program, you need to find an executive sponsor who:

- ☑ Recognizes that data is a critical corporate asset, as important as people, capital, or equipment.
- ☑ Recruits and cultivates other data-driven leaders on the executive team.
- ☑ Knows the company and its processes, is widely respected, and expects to stay in her position for the foreseeable future.
- ☑ Evangelizes the importance of data and analytics to the organization and invests time, money, and people to achieve that vision.
- ☑ Publicly designates a data warehouse as a certified source for decisions, and personally uses that data to make or validate decisions.
- ☑ Assigns a key lieutenant to oversee the analytics program who spends a significant portion of his time each week working with analytical leaders and their teams.

☑ Leads interference for the analytics program, including enlisting other executives to fund the program and convincing them to assign their top analysts to work with the analytical team.

☑ Evangelizes analytics to mid-level managers who often serve as a chokepoint for data workflows in the organization and front-line workers who must learn new analytical tools and processes.

☑ Helps create an executive committee within an analytical center of excellence that prioritizes projects, approves funding, and reviews roadmaps.

☑ Establishes a performance measurement system in which people and teams are regularly evaluated based on their performance against strategically-aligned metrics.

☑ Understands what analytical capabilities to outsource and which to keep inhouse.

☑ Understands the limits of analytical models and how they can go wrong.

☑ Understands the limits of intuition and makes decisions based on a combination of intuition and data.

Obviously, strong executive leadership is critical to the success of an analytics program. Finding the right sponsor to kick off a program is critical. Once the program gains critical mass, you need an steering committee comprised of sponsors from multiple business units that shepherds the analytics program to its full maturity. (See Chapter 9.)

COMMENTARY FROM ANALYTICAL LEADERS

COLSON: When your analytics team continually adds business value, you gain the trust and confidence of executives, and you no longer need to justify each decision. For example, I once negotiated a seven-figure deal with an analytics vendor. The only thing left to do was put a signature on the contract. So, I met with my CEO, told him about the deal, and pushed the contract across the table for him to sign. He pushed it back, saying: "If you think this deal will make us more effective, then sign the contract and make it happen. We trust you to use good judgment."

MEASURING SUCCESS. I haven't found any explicit metrics that accurately capture the analytics team's contribution to a company. And that's ironic since we are the group that empirically measures everything! In some cases, you can quantify the impact of a specific initiative through A/B testing, but in general, it is difficult to measure the value of knowledge generated by an analytics program.

So, I tend to measure our success based on the level of confidence and trust that I perceive business leaders have in the analytics team. Do they trust our data enough to make critical decisions with it? Do they come to the analytics team for advice? Do they treat the analytics team as a partner? Do they recognize the contributions of the analytics team during business review meetings? Admittedly, this is more of a gut feel than something you can quantify. But, it all comes down to delivering value continuously. If you do that, you build confidence and trust.

LEONARD: When I join a company or work with a new department, the first thing I do is to roll up my sleeves and learn the business. I don't go to the finance group and say, "I'm going to build a dashboard for you." Rather, I say, "Let's sit down and look at your balance sheet." After I've gained sufficient domain knowledge, I start working with the business people to explore their business fundamentals with them.

For instance, I might say to a finance executive, "Let's look at your journals and explore the profitability of account items outside the balance sheet." At that point, they look at me and say, "Are you a technologist or an accountant?" That's when I know I'm succeeding. I work hard to talk the language of business. The more you discuss technology, the less the business listens to you. I never talk about star schemas, facts and dimensions, or data warehouses, ETL, or Hadoop with business people. Those mean nothing to them. I focus on business problems.

I started my career as a hard-core technologist, but I discovered that doesn't get you very far in the business world. To succeed, you need to be a really good salesman and marketer as well as a technologist who delivers high quality applications on time and under budget. You have to be the total package.

You also have to think of your team as a business and your solutions as products. In my world, there is no distinction between business and IT. We simply deliver business solutions. I don't even consider myself an information technology (IT) professional anymore. If you're just a technologist who enables the business, you're viewed as a cost center, not a strategic partner.

TAYLOR: We've been fortunate at Blue KC to have an executive team that understands the importance of managing data properly and informing decision makers with insights gleaned from data. They know they can't achieve the company's strategic vision without investing heavily in data. But it hasn't always been a cakewalk.

In 2003, it became clear that our existing data warehouse wasn't working out. It hadn't been designed from an enterprise perspective—it was basically a data dump of our major claims system and didn't provide a comprehensive or integrated view of the enterprise spanning member, provider, actuarial, underwriting, and clinical data.

However, instead of panning the data warehouse, our executives decided to double down and build a new one. And that's even before we paid off the existing data warehouse, which was only three years old. They created a new data warehousing team and put me in charge, reporting directly to the CIO, with the COO as the executive business sponsor. This was no longer an IT initiative. We recruited the right people from both business and IT to serve on the team, and we quickly delivered results. That data warehouse has been a big success.

FROM DATA WAREHOUSING TO ANALYTICS. We had a tougher time when we launched our analytical initiative in 2010. There were many executives on the team who didn't understand why we weren't more successful with analytics, since we were spending a lot of time and resources on data warehousing. Although our data warehouse delivered the right data, it didn't generate the analytical models that we needed to run the business. Our business units had independently sourced a variety of analytical applications that they ran against data that they pulled from our data warehouse. These applications came with built-in analytical models that did things like score member propensity to utilize various medical services or suffer complications from surgery. Many had overlapping functionality and generated conflicting results.

So, I put together a business plan that demonstrated how consolidating analytics onto a unified platform run by a single group would save the company significant money and provide a single version of analytical truth. Some business unit heads were resistant because they thought they would lose their analysts. Other executives thought that the data warehouse should already be delivering analytics and didn't know why the company had to fund a separate program.

However, once executives saw that program would pay for itself, they jumped on board, and we quickly launched the program. Although we sold the analytics program solely on the cost-savings of consolidating analytics onto a single, integrated platform, the executives understood that most of the value from the investment would come from insights generated by the new models.

FROM A COST CENTER TO PROFIT CENTER. Early on, the executive team recognized that other health plans might be interested in this type of analytical solution. So, they decided to commercialize it through a subsidiary called Cobalt Talon, which now offers both data warehousing and analytical products as well as consulting services to health plans. Blue KC is the subsidiary's first customer, and I was appointed its president and COO in June, 2012. It's been rewarding to transform our data warehousing and analytics initiative from a cost-center to a profit center. This is what it's all about!

O'CONNOR: Even with executives that understand the value proposition of data and analytics, we have to regularly quantify and qualify the value of analytics so they can understand what they are getting from their investments.

For example, we have defined key performance indicators

(KPIs) on the data asset itself—how much data we have, what are the growth rates, how often are different data streams processed and for what reason, how many business KPIs are now reported using the data asset, and so on. We display real-time counters of the data as it flows into the system. We trace test messages at every step of our data assembly line: from mobile devices to edge node servers to scribe servers to Hadoop file systems to Oracle data warehouses and to dashboard displays. We statistically model the data asset to show its history, identify anomalies in behavior, and predict future growth.

We also qualify the progress of our 'smart data' strategy by arming executives and employees with success stories and proof points. We quickly learned that data visualization is very important to help spread the word about the success of our 'smart data' initiative. For instance, we built heatmaps that layer different types of activity data—such as search requests, drive probes, traffic – on top of street maps. We built animations of that activity to show how it changes over time from city to city. These visualizations are eye-catching and highlight the type of data in our system.

By arming our executives with these KPIs and visualizations, we enlighten executives about the nature and value of our data asset and ensure their continued support.

 **INGLE:** The executives at Kelley Blue Book were receptive to using analytics, but they didn't exactly know how to implement it or how it could transform the way the company does business. Fortunately, they brought the right people together at the right time, and our analytics strategy unfolded in quick order.

Shawn Hushman, who is vice president of enterprise analytics, and I were the primary drivers. Shawn has an extensive background in predictive and Web analytics and has worked in a range of industries. I came from Capital One Auto Finance, where we integrated analytics into the loan origination process for consumers.

To get the ball rolling, we convinced the top executives of both the upside of embracing analytics and downside of not doing so. They bought into the idea relatively quickly. It really wasn't a hard sell. The executives knew that Kelley Blue Book needed to change, and were looking for the way to get there. The market was moving fast and our competitors were getting more sophisticated. At the time, we published vehicle values monthly, but this was no longer sufficient. The executives recognized that Kelley Blue Book needed to deliver more localized, timely, and relevant vehicle values to stay competitive. So, they empowered Shawn and me to make this happen.

SUMMARY

It's been said that fruit doesn't fall far from the tree. Executives weaned on data-driven business diets become analytical leaders who use data to drive their organizations in the right direction. Thus, it's important to find or cultivate business executives to spearhead the analytical effort. Without executive nurturing, analytics cannot thrive. In the next chapter, we'll see how selling analytics to executives often involves delivering a quick win reinforced with a change management program that bakes analytics into the culture of the organization.

CHAPTER 7

HOW DO YOU GAIN MOMENTUM FOR AN ANALYTICS PROGRAM?

The hardest part about running an analytics program is getting started. An analytics program is like a giant flywheel that takes enormous effort to get moving, but once it does, it creates its own momentum and becomes hard to stop.

Most of the analytical leaders profiled in this book emphasize the importance of a quick win to gain momentum and credibility for the program. Kurt Thearling says that the first thing he does with a new client is to find a "meaningful" problem that executives care about. Tim Leonard talks about using quick wins to change perceptions of the IT department and gain credibility with the business. And Darren Taylor emphasizes the importance of delivering a few applications during the course of implementing a new data warehouse to give executives a taste of things to come.

By definition, a quick win delivers something that the business values in a shorter-than-expected period of time. In essence, it's a wakeup call to the business that what they thought about technology and technologists no longer applies. The message of a quick win is: analytics is no longer a black hole into which money goes and nothing comes out; rather, it's a critical resource that can answer long sought-after questions, solve problems, and improve performance.

Crafting the quick win. There are many ways to craft a quick win. The catch is that you usually have to break or bend the rules to succeed. For instance, Tim Leonard put his new team through a six week "death march" to achieve breakthrough results that changed the reputation of the IT department at U.S. Xpress. He also broke his own rules and built an independent data mart instead of an enterprise data warehouse to run his new application.

Other analytical leaders have executed quick wins by adopting non-standard technologies, such as analytical appliances to turbo-charge performance, or cloud-based solutions to accelerate deployment. Others have served notice by replacing detailed, tabular reports with visually appealing dashboards, or deploying sexy iPad apps to augment Web-based applications. In all cases, business people began seeing analytical teams as a critical partner in their success rather than a perpetual roadblo   ck to getting things done.

Curse of success. One problem with quick wins is that they can create an avalanche of demand that overwhelms an analytics program. As Tim Leonard points out, analytical leaders need to be ready for the "curse of success" by establishing an executive-level governance committee that prioritizes requests for analytical services and takes the political heat off the analytical director. They also need to create a plan for scaling the analytical architecture to handle more users and data. Finally, they need to watch for jealous colleagues and neglected business heads who might torpedo the program before it gets off the ground. Without a quick response to the hazards of a quick win, analytical leaders can quickly return the doghouse.

MANAGING CHANGE

Once the analytical flywheel starts moving, it's important to sustain the momentum until it becomes baked into the culture of the organization. This requires a change management strategy, which is critical to the success of any analytics program. For instance, Nokia executives have embarked on a change management crusade to ensure all employees understand the importance of data to the company's future. And Dan Ingle says change management is the key to getting business analysts at Kelley Blue Book to fully embrace quantitative methods for forecasting vehicle values.

Empathize. The first tenet of any change management program is to recognize that the smallest change in an analytical process or output (i.e., the way a report looks or feels) is disconcerting to most workers. Some may lash out at the analytical team, even though the change gives them better information with which to do their jobs. These people often feel they don't have time to learn something like the new tool or fear the change might erode their responsibilities or cause them to lose their competitive edge. Before introducing change, analytical leaders need to empathize with the business users whose decision-making lives they are about to throw into disarray. They also must brace for a backlash and remain professional at all costs. They know that when people become tense or angry, it's usually because they feel threatened.

Manage expectations. One way to reduce the stress of change is to manage expectations. That means communicating early and often about changes—before they happen, when they happen, and after they happen. Analytical leaders must persuade top executives to trumpet the rationale and benefits of any major analytical change. And they need to devise a comprehensive marketing and communications plan that identifies target audiences affected by the change. As part of the plan, they need to devise unique messages for each target group and deliver those messages using the most appropriate channels of communication, including Web, email, company meetings, company newsletters, etc. In essence, an analytical leader has to be a savvy marketer who understands branding, promotions, and campaigns.

Multi-touch support. But change management goes beyond messaging and communications. It's critical to offer plenty of support to help people migrate from the old environment to the new one. Some people need more hand-holding than others. Executives often require one-on-one tutorials before they feel comfortable switching to the new analytical environment, while managers and knowledge workers may need formal training supplemented with online or phone support that provides quick answers to their questions.

Track usage. Finally, you can't manage change if you don't know how people are using a new system or application, so it's critical to track usage.

Analytical leaders first establish a baseline for analytical usage and then track the uptake during roll out of a new environment. If usage dips below expected levels, analytical leaders take quick action. They visit departments where usage is low and ask questions. They try to find out what users like and don't like about the new application and make appropriate changes. Analytical leaders know that first impressions can spell the difference between the success and failure of a new system, so they diligently track usage to ensure that system changes have the desired impact.

In the end, analytical leaders need to build a bridge from an old analytical environment to a new one. Although some employees will race across the bridge and wonder why the analytical team took so long to build it, the majority of corporate citizens will cross the bridge in due time. However, an obstinate few will hold out until the bitter end. Analytical leaders need to identify the holdouts in advance, especially if they are executives. It's important to listen to their concerns, quell their anxieties about the change, and provide sufficient one-on-one support. That's the carrot. The stick, which most analytical leaders eventually wield, is to turn off the old environment and force users to convert to the new one.

COMMENTARY FROM ANALYTICAL LEADERS

QUICK WINS

THEARLING: The best way to gain momentum for analytics is to solve a meaningful problem for executives, even if it is a small one. And it's best to solve a problem they already care about, rather than one that they should care about.

For example, when I started as head of decision sciences at Vertex Business Services, a business process outsourcer, I asked my boss, the Chief Operating Officer (COO), how many employees he had. He didn't know the answer, at least not exactly. And it turns out this was a source of angst for him. So, I dug into the question with my head of data management and in a week had an answer for him. We built a little data mart, using QlikTech's QlikView, that pulled data from our human resources and payroll systems. It wasn't beautiful but it provided the necessary answer.

Other executives looked at the data and asked questions, such as "How many people do we pay that don't work for us?" and "What employees don't have a boss?" Fortunately, we populated the application with enough data to answer those questions, too. Interestingly, we discovered that we were paying several people who no longer worked at the company, which was of keen interest to the CFO! We eventually merged the data from this application into our standard reporting system, which delivers monthly dashboards to executives.

This was all pretty simple stuff, but by answering a meaningful question, we quickly became indispensable. I've done the same thing with clients. I help them pick a meaningful question, and then quickly conduct data analysis to get the answer. That one question turns into five questions, which turns into 25 questions and so on. If your first question isn't meaningful, you don't get the momentum and the credibility you need to succeed.

 **LEONARD:** Once you get executive buy in, then you have to deliver something meaningful and do it quickly. For instance, the first thing we did when I arrived at U.S. Xpress was to build a dashboard that tracks the amount of time our trucks spent idling each day. Our COO remarked, "I've been here 25 years and no one has ever given me this data." That dashboard got me in the door and gave me some credibility to pitch other things. I had taken the first all-important step.

DEATH MARCH. It took us six weeks to build that dashboard, which was a death march. My team worked quadruple time. Otherwise, it would have taken months to finish, which I knew wasn't going to fly. The business didn't have a lot of respect for us or want to engage us. We had to do something dramatic to get their attention and change their perceptions.

To ensure a quick turnaround, we scoped the problem narrowly and avoided getting bogged down in architecture. We only captured relevant data elements out of hundreds emitted by onboard truck sensors and systems, even though we knew we might need the rest of the elements at a later point.

We didn't want to boil the ocean. Although I'm a firm believer in the need for an enterprise data warehouse, in this case, we decided to build a data mart directly off the source systems. I knew the executives would use the idle application to make four or five decisions at most. So we kept it simple, pulled only the data we needed, and delivered the application quickly.

Our quick win gave us instant credibility. Business heads lined up to talk with us. We quickly ended up with many new project proposals, which represented an overwhelming amount of work, but it was better than being ignored. I told the CEO that I could only build a small set of projects with my current resources. He really wanted four additional projects, so he increased our headcount and gave us the necessary funds and asked us to deliver the projects in several months. And this was back during the depth of the recession. Our CEO wanted all the IT projects completed before the recession ended so the business could take off when the economy rebounded. He is truly a visionary CEO. I don't know anyone else in his position who thought or did the same thing.

THE CURSE OF SUCCESS. The hardest part about our new workload was that the executives expected us to deliver the same miracle with each new project. That's the downside of a quick win—the curse of success. They never saw how hard we worked to deliver the first dashboard. We were like ducks: above water, we were calm and cool, but below we were paddling like hell! To bolster the morale of my troops in the face of this colossal workload, I told them that our quick win earned us a ticket to play the game, but these new projects entitled us to score points. And believe it or not, the team came through and we delivered all but two of the projects on time. It was tough year, but gratifying in the end.

These weren't small projects either. One was a customer relationship management (CRM) application, which executives wanted us to deliver in less than half a year. No one thought we could do it. They laughed at us. Even the sales team said it would never happen. But guess what? We delivered that application in five months and three days, and it became a huge success. We delivered six projects on time and under budget, so, on the whole we were quite successful. We ended up working with nearly every department in the company, whereas in the first 25 years of the company, the IT department had only worked with a few successfully.

TAYLOR: It's important to deliver some applications even before you finish the project to cement executives' commitment to the program. Gaining credibility at an early stage comes in handy when you hit unanticipated snags.

For example, before we finished implementing our analytical infrastructure (i.e., an analytical data mart) at Blue KC, we delivered a financial dashboard on the iPad that was a big hit among executives. We also delivered a self-service portal while building our data warehouse that enabled physicians and hospitals to view all the claims they had with us, which they had never been able to do before. That application probably consumed two to three percent of the total project time, but it made our network providers happy and eliminated phone calls that consumed a lot of staff time.

Once we got further along and built out the membership subject area in the data warehouse, we implemented an analytical application that predicts annual healthcare costs for every member. Several departments—underwriting, medical management, and actuary—had been asking for this predictive risk scoring application for years, but we never had integrated data to feed the models. The model helped us identify people upfront who needed disease or case management services, instead of finding out after the fact, when claims were submitted. It also enabled us to more accurately and efficiently set renewal rates for employer groups.

All these interim applications provided a real win for us. They cemented executive support and gave us additional momentum.

CHANGE MANAGEMENT

O'CONNOR: A major challenge we face is selling analytics to the entire organization. As I mentioned earlier, our executives' vision is dependent on analytics and 'smart data', but now we need to get all Nokia employees around the world to buy into that vision as well. To do that, we need to master cultural change. But changing people is hard.

Changing people's behaviors and attitudes is not unlike trying to get your kids to eat something they don't like. We found an instructive research study that examined how to get kids to eat peas. The study evaluated various options for getting kids to eat peas, including issuing orders or edicts, explaining the health benefits in a logical way, and offering them an incentive, such as a bowl of ice cream. The study showed that the most effective option is to socialize them with children who like peas. In other words, children will eat their peas if their friends eat them.

To apply this concept at Nokia, we are changing the stories we tell employees, and creating communities for employees to interact with peers about their experiences with analytics. We are building a culture in which people naturally assume that data is critical to the company's strategy. We are doing this by continuously communicating the importance of creating a global data repository and harnessing data to create a new generation of Nokia products.

COMMUNITY BUILDING. One program that we launched to help us drive the change is called "Community Building and Communications." To foster the right culture, this program publishes a newsletter and blog and holds meetings between the centralized analytics team and the distributed application teams. It also maintains a wiki that documents analytical artifacts in the company, such as operational dashboards, business KPIs, models, and visualizations. Additionally, the program uses corporate social networks to foster community. We deployed an analytics community using VMware's Socialcast collaboration tool and in the first week, several hundred people participated, many posting articles about their analytics projects and asking for feedback, which they got in droves. We believe that communication and community building will help showcase the benefits of analytics and increase adoption.

The second program is called "Simplifying the Use of the Data Asset." This program invests time and money into making our data asset easy to access and use. Among our initiatives here is the development of a data catalog. This is a menu of available data available and its characteristics. We've also recruited our data science team to profile the data, share interesting insights about it, and predict how the data asset will evolve in the future.

INGLE: One reason Kelley Blue Book struggled to apply analytics to vehicle valuations before I arrived is that it didn't invest enough in change management. By that, I mean the impact a new solution would have on business users. Today, we work hard to establish tight working relationships among three groups of people: data developers who manage data and create reports; statisticians who create forecasts and analytical models; and vehicle valuation analysts who use the output of statistical models to estimate the value of new and used vehicles. Our solutions have had a big impact on how everyone does their jobs.

For example, to get the vehicle valuation analysts comfortable with the change, we spent considerable time educating them about predictive modeling. We explained how a predictive model works: how it takes sales transactions and other key data feeds and uses advanced mathematics to forecast what a car will be worth next week, next month, or next year. Our valuation analysts are analytical in nature, so they learned quickly. We encouraged them to sit with the statisticians and learn as much as they could, and the statisticians were happy to oblige. This helped analysts see what data feeds the models and how the models interpret that data. They learned how statisticians trim outliers, combine multiple models to generate output with a better fit, and consolidate data to measure the impact of mileage or optional equipment. We tried to demystify the black box of statistical modeling so that our analysts could become comfortable reviewing and validating statistical output as they develop vehicle forecasts.

We made sure we gave analysts time to ease into the new process. We didn't create models, turn them on, and shove the statistical forecasts down their throats. Instead, we bolted the statistical models to the analysts' existing method of creating pricing forecasts. As the analysts have become more comfortable with statistical processes, they have allowed the models to do more of the heavy lifting. This has freed them to explore anomalies with statisticians and generate additional market insights.

SUMMARY

To gain momentum for an analytics program, analytical leaders need to master two arts: the quick win and change management. The analytical leaders who succeed in these endeavors usually exhibit ample sales, marketing, and project management skills. In other words, they know how to manage and motivate people. Of course, the people they know best are analysts and data developers. Defining the roles and responsibilities of these analytical workers and how to recruit them are the subjects of the next chapter.

CHAPTER 8

WHAT IS AN ANALYST AND WHERE DO YOU FIND THEM?

It's impossible to do analytics without analysts. That's obvious. But there is a lot of confusion about what an analyst is and does. As Darren Taylor points out, human resources departments often indiscriminately assign the title "analyst" to many positions that span both the business and IT departments. Even the analytical leaders profiled in this book use the title "analyst" to describe a number of different roles and positions. As an industry, we need to crystallize the definition of analyst so that organizations better understand the people resources required to deliver effective analytical solutions.

So, I'm going to put a proverbial stake in the ground. Based on my research, there are two categories of analysts. There are *data developers* who build things and true *analysts* who discover things. Although these are distinct roles, they are often merged within a single position, sometimes formally, but many times informally. Compounding the confusion, there are several types of data developers and analysts.

DATA DEVELOPERS

At a high level, data developers build data warehouses, data marts, and master data management systems as well as complex reports and dashboards that require custom coding. In most companies, data developers are known as business intelligence (BI) developers or professionals. Unfortunately, BI has an IT connotation that doesn't always align with the nature of what data developers do. So, following the lead of Eric Colson, I now use the term data developer to describe this type of position.

Some organizations hire a raft of specialists to develop analytical applications and house them in a corporate BI or data warehousing (DW) team. These BI/DW specialists—or data developers as I call them—include report developers, DW modelers, data acquisition developers, DW architects, requirements specialists, data administrators, and quality assurance testers. A few organizations ask individual data developers to do all of the above tasks within a narrow business domain while coordinating their data modeling activities to ensure alignment. (See Eric Colson's concept of the "spanner" in Chapter 11.)

Most organizations have data developers at both corporate and departmental levels of the organization. Corporate data developers build the enterprise data warehouse, logical data marts, and cross-functional reports and dashboards, while departmental data developers build departmental reports and dashboards, satisfy ad hoc report requests, specify local requirements for enterprise projects. Sometimes, the departmental developers also build local data marts, if they have unique data that no other group needs to access.

ANALYSTS

In comparison, true analysts discover patterns and anomalies in data using ad hoc query, visual discovery, and machine learning tools. Although data developers generally work with data in a data warehouse, analysts use any data necessary to answer business questions, including data from the data warehouse, operational systems, Hadoop, and external sources. Although there are many types of data developers, there are only four types of analysts: business analysts, data analysts, statisticians (or analytical modelers), and data scientists.

Business analysts. Business analysts often use Excel to create and evaluate plans and answer ad hoc questions from an executive or manager that can't be addressed by a standard report or dashboard. They generally have a degree from a business school, possess strong quantitative skills, and report to the head of a functional area, such as sales, marketing, or finance.

Data analysts. Data analysts sit squarely between the data developer and analyst communities, as well as between business and IT. As Kurt Thearling describes below, data analysts are the keepers of analytical data. They provide access to data and document and organize it so business users can quickly find the information they need. Good data analysts have many of the skills of a business analyst or statistician but prefer to organize the data for others to use. They often work closely with data administrators in the IT department who ensure that data is properly formatted, stored, cleansed, and secured.

Statisticians. Statisticians have formal training in statistics and know how to use a data mining workbench. Many also know how to write SQL and work closely with the raw data. Statisticians build descriptive and predictive models that are the heart and soul of advanced analytics. Some companies embed statisticians in functional departments, while others centralize them to foster greater collaboration. Many companies recruit statisticians from academia and social sciences.

Data scientists. Data scientists combine the skills of a business analyst, statistician, and Java developer. In other words, data scientists are a rare breed, but highly sought-after by companies that have implemented Hadoop, including Nokia (see below.) Data scientists specialize in analyzing unstructured data, such as Web traffic and social media, although they are by no means restricted to it. As Hadoop matures and provides higher-level methods for accessing data, the role of the data scientist will morph into that of a business analyst or statistician.

SUPERUSERS

Many business analysts—especially those who work at small or mid-size companies or who are embedded in functional units—also perform the work of a departmental data developer. That is, they write departmental reports and dashboards and handle ad hoc requests from business users. And conversely, many departmental report writers often conduct exploratory analyses to answer time-sensitive questions from business users.

When business analysts or departmental report developers do each other's work, I call them "superusers." These people augment the corporate BI/DW team by handling local requests for custom reports and providing input on requirements for enterprise data projects. Many also serve on analytical governance committees that coordinate analytical projects and development across departments.

Although superusers are quite valuable, it's not always wise for an analytical professional to do double duty. Executives pay business analysts good money to answer critical questions, such as "What will be the impact if we raise prices by 5%?" Or "What will be the impact on our profits if we acquire company A?" So, asking a business analyst to spend most of their time writing ad hoc reports for departmental colleagues is not always a profitable use of their time. Although small organizations may not be able to afford both departmental report developers and business analysts, larger companies often create distinct positions for these roles. This gives them top value for their hiring dollar and helps retain business analysts who don't want to get stuck doing lower value work. However, Eric Colson makes a case in Chapter 11 that combining both developer and analyst functions in one person is exactly the right approach.

Hopefully, dividing the analyst community into two main branches: data developers and true analysts provides some clarity around who analysts are and what they do. For the most part, our analytical leaders align with this categorization.

COMMENTARY FROM ANALYTICAL LEADERS

WHAT IS AN ANALYST?

TAYLOR: At Blue KC, we don't have a crisp definition of the term "analyst." We have a lot of positions with the word "analyst" in the title, but the people in these positions are often glorified report writers. They tend to take orders from business users who prescribe in detail what they want. Report writing is a valuable service, but it does not involve discovery and synthesis which is what real analysts do.

For instance, we created the position of a "health data analyst" to focus on the business side of health data. Unfortunately, over the years, the people in this role have become report writers. We also have systems analysts, requirements analysts, and other types of analysts that have nothing to do with data discovery or exploration. We need to work with our human resources and business departments to apply a more rigorous definition to the term "analyst" when creating job titles. And we need to rescue our analysts from serving as report writers.

THEARLING: At Capital One, we had three kinds of analysts: 1) business analysts, who worked mostly with tools like Excel and had graduate degrees in business administration, 2) data analysts who provided access to data from the multitude of systems across the company, and 3) statisticians who sit between the business analysts and data analysts and turn data into business value. Statisticians are comfortable with raw data, but prefer to spend most of their time discovering patterns in the data.

DATA ANALYSTS. In a large organization with complex data, it's critically important to have data analysts to curate and source data so that business analysts and statisticians don't have to waste their time trying to find data to analyze. At Capital One, there were some people who had the fantasy of making data so easy to access that we no longer needed data analysts. Although that is a worthy objective, it's a hard to achieve in a large, complex, and dynamic data environment.

In addition to supporting access to the data, data analysts also capture and know the meaning of the data. This goes beyond basic metadata management. It's not just getting someone to record that a credit score field is an integer that ranges from 350 to 850. The more important information is the tribal knowledge that says, "From March 2007 to April 2008, the upper range of the field is 836 because someone made a data processing mistake." We captured this type of metadata in a wiki that allowed free-form text and multiple contributors.

STATISTICIANS. Statisticians are also a special breed. I liken them to fine furniture makers who can look at a pile of wood, feel its grain, know which pieces to pull, and which of their 40 chisels to use to create a desired shape. They are true craftsmen.

But a statistician doesn't deliver high value right away. It takes years of training and experience. They are like woodworkers who serve many years as an apprentice before becoming a fine craftsman. Through on-the-job training, a statistician learns which tools and data to use when crafting models.

Interestingly, if a statistician switches jobs and moves to a company in the same industry and field, he still needs several months before he can deliver significant value. Although, credit scores look the same at Citibank and Chase, statisticians need time to acclimate to subtle differences in the data at each organization and how each organization uses data.

PRODUCTION SUPPORT. It's also important to have people who manage the process of putting models into production. They aren't analysts, but they play a critical role in helping companies reap the value of analytical models.

For example, when I ran the decision sciences consulting practice at Vertex, I had a client management and sales support team that did everything from presales and project management to systems integration and production operations. They pulled everything together to ensure we delivered services to clients as promised. They coordinated the data administrators and analysts to make sure we delivered data and models on time, and they figured out how to implement the statistical models. For example, if the goal of a campaign was to target outbound calls for debt collection, they worked to generate the call center scripts and figured out how to hook the analytics into an automated dialer. These folks were our jack of all trades who did the nuts and bolts of putting analytics into production. They were critical to our success.

COLSON: In a data-driven culture, the term "analyst" doesn't have a black and white definition. That's because people in almost every department do analysis of some kind. In this sense, an analyst is less of a role and more of a function.

Within the data team, you have two types of analysts. On one hand, there are data developers who shepherd data from source to insight and build reports and dashboards. On the other, there are data scientists and statisticians who employ more sophisticated statistical methods to generate insights.

DATA DEVELOPERS. In a fast-moving company, it is hard to separate analysis from development. Good data developers have deep knowledge of the data and its lineage and all the intricacies about how data was acquired and transformed. In fact, good data developers often define what data gets generated in the first place. This knowledge enables them to build great reports and dashboards that provide great visibility into the business. It also equips them to answer ad hoc questions from the business that can't be answered with standard reports and dashboards.

Although ad hoc work is traditionally what business analysts do, I find that giving data developers this responsibility gives them the deep business context they need to build really good data models, ETL programs, reports, and dashboards. The reverse is also true. Analysts that develop reports do better analysis because they understand the nuances of relevant business processes and the data that underlies them. Moreover, most data developers love analytical work and find it the most enjoyable part of their jobs.

DATA SCIENTISTS. Besides data developers, you also need analysts who create predictive models, develop algorithms, and run experiments. These so-called data scientists usually have PhDs or Master's degrees in math or statistics or an advanced degree from a quantitatively-oriented computer science program. Most are fluent in R, SAS, or Matlab and know how to access relational databases using SQL and Hadoop using Python or other languages.

INGLE: Kelley Blue Book has analysts across the enterprise. We have a small team of data analysts who acquire and scrub data and a team of about ten analysts who create vehicle values. In addition, my colleague, Shawn Hushman, who is Vice President of the Enterprise Analytics team, manages a handful of statisticians who create vehicle valuation models and more than a dozen analysts who forecast Web traffic.

DATA ANALYSTS. Our data analysts are experts in the raw material. Basically, they know everything about the data we acquire. They know where it comes from, how it is derived, where the skeletons are buried, and where it goes. Their job is to get the data others need. The other analysts consult with them to find the best data possible for their analyses. If we create a new product or item, they have to find the data to support it, even if that means acquiring the data from outside sources. And then they have to extract and prepare the data for actual use; often a tall order, given the lack of data standards in the automotive industry.

VEHICLE VALUATION ANALYSTS. Our valuation analysts produce the value of vehicles across all makes and models in all regions on a weekly basis. They are responsible for setting the dollar figures for every car you search for on our Web site, so their work is the most visible element of our commercial offerings. They don't develop the models or produce the forecasts—they aren't SAS coders, for example—rather, they evaluate the accuracy of models created by our enterprise analytics team.

Interestingly, we didn't have SAS modelers until about four years ago. Before then, the vehicle valuation analysts estimated prices entirely on their own, using a combination of industry expertise, intuition, and sample data sets. We've been inserting analytical models into the existing valuation process at a moderate pace and that transition is still going on today. Our goal is to continually increase the degree and percentage of our published vehicle values that are driven completely by statistical models.

When we first began hiring statisticians to produce forecasts our vehicle valuation analysts felt threatened. They were concerned about job security and questioned whether a model could forecast the market better than they could. Today, they recognize that the models produce effective forecasts, and they no longer fear being replaced. They understand that the models free them to work on other projects. With the advent of the statistical models, they now produce more work in less time with greater effectiveness.

SHARED GOALS. We foster a close partnership between the statisticians and vehicle valuation analysts by giving them the same goals, objectives and performance metrics. Essentially, we incent both groups to increase the effectiveness of our statistical forecasts. To do this, we keep two scorecards: one that tracks what the statistical models predicted, and the other which tracks the values that analysts actually published. And then using hold-out samples, we compare both to what really happened and score how close they came to reality. We pay particular attention to instances when analysts override a statistical model. Both groups are accountable for the accuracy of both sets of scores.

This joint accountability fosters a close relationship and two-way exchange of information. For instance, when analysts see something in the model output that seems off, they talk to the statistician to see if a weighting or variable needs tweaking. Here, analysts teach the statisticians about the auto industry. But, statisticians also teach the analysts about the nuances of predictive modeling. This partnership makes the models more effective and reduces the number of overrides. The more we can rely on the models, the more efficient we can be.

STATISTICIANS. Shawn populates our statistical team with people from a mix of academic backgrounds. These include statisticians, applied mathematicians, econometricians, operational researchers, physicists and social scientists. Each discipline approaches statistical problems from a slightly different perspective, which generates lots of productive debate and an academic environment that statisticians enjoy. Our team was initially overweighted with statisticians, so Shawn hired a few econometricians to balance things out. The team enjoys working together, and they learn a lot from each other.

WHERE DO YOU FIND ANALYSTS?

O'CONNOR: Our biggest challenge with analytics is finding people to do the analysis. A true data scientist has a combination of computer engineering ability, mathematical and statistical knowledge, an insatiable curiosity, and an understanding of what will be interesting and useful. I'm sure many people have seen the McKinsey report that predicts we will have a significant deficit of these specialists over the next few years. We are starting to see schools work toward putting together material to provide future students with the right balance of engineering, mathematical, and cultural studies.

For the most part, we find that we need to train data scientists internally. We create mini-SWAT teams that blend people with different skills to create a composite data scientist. Here, we pair people coming out of academia who have statistical skills with people who have been in the industry for several years solving data-centric business problems. For example, we have a summer intern who is working toward her Doctorate in Quantitative Psychology and has the statistical skills and cultural knowledge to be a data scientist. In her first few weeks at work, she has already produced interesting insights around the adoption and usage of Nokia's music service. So we are bridging the data science gap with these mini-SWAT teams and so far, it is working well.

RUDIN: I look for analysts with a strong business background and an analytical mindset, not just a PhD in statistics. Some people use the term data scientist to describe these people, but I think that term focuses too much on their technical skills.

BUSINESS EXPERIENCE. Since I've always tried to apply computer science to business, I have a definite bias towards people who have a good understanding of analytics and a strong knowledge of business, and can work in both worlds. I certainly hire people who possess an analytical mindset and core analytical skills, but I look for people who also have spent time as a business or operations manager. I want people who have a sense of the business side of analytics, not just the mathematical side. These people can have a much bigger impact.

The head of Zynga's analyst team has a PhD in economics. He knows the core statistical stuff, and he ran a whole team of data-driven consultants at a prior company. But like me, he's not a trained analyst. I took one statistics course in college, and the rest I picked up as I went along. I'm more of a business guy who thinks analytically, and that's helped me understand the value of having both business and analytical skills.

EVANGELISTS VERSUS ORACLES. My motto is: hire evangelists, not oracles. You want people who are passionate about using analytics to change the business, who know how to ask the right questions, and approach things differently. We don't want people who say, "Ask me a question, and I'll answer it." Evangelists are proactive, oracles are reactive. My ideal candidate is a product marketing manager who has a degree in math, physics, economics, or computer science and wants to do analytics.

Let me give you an example of the type of analyst I would NOT hire. We invited a guest speaker to talk to our analytics team who has PhD's on top of PhD's and is clearly a very smart guy. He analyzed a popular football video game that had hundreds of built-in plays. He discovered an inverse correlation between the number of different plays people use in the game and the number of months they play. People who used only three to four plays had a higher retention rate than people who used dozens of plays. I raised my hand and said, "That's counterintuitive. You would think the person who uses many different plays enjoys a richer game experience compared to someone who uses the same plays all the time, which would get rote and boring." Then, I asked, "Why would fewer plays lead to longer retention?" He said, "I don't know, I'm just the analyst. I only find the patterns."

That was a really bad answer! I want an analyst who, after discovering such a pattern, would devise a few hypotheses about what causes the pattern and then find ways to test the hypotheses. Someone with an analytical background plus business savvy is more likely to come up with good hypotheses than someone with an analytical background only. A pure mathematician won't create a hypothesis, but a business person will.

Afterwards, just for fun, I had my team brainstorm ideas about what caused the pattern that our guest speaker discovered. We came up with dozens of hypotheses and, equally important, potential ways to test them. One hypothesis was that there might be three or four plays that win most of the time and so highly competitive players stick with those. Another was that some plays are easier to access than others. The bottom line is that it takes creativity and business sense to come up with hypotheses, not just analytical prowess.

BRILLIANT BUT USELESS. The challenge with hiring statisticians without business skills is that that they often come up with brilliant answers to questions that people don't care about. For example, one of Zynga's analysts figured out the optimal time that Zynga should launch a new game to minimize cannibalization of its existing games. It was a clever idea full of brilliant mathematics. But from a business perspective, it was useless, because game developers don't release games before they are ready, and they don't delay shipping a completed game because a competitor might swoop in and take market share. So the analyst came up with a brilliant model that the game studios would never use. Analysis without business sense is often useless.

When someone asks me how they can become a better analyst, I usually recommend that they improve their business skills. Specifically, I recommend that they take a class in presentation skills, which will help them more than taking a class on the latest statistical techniques. With solid presentation skills, they can better describe their insights to others and persuade them to act on those insights.

SUMMARY

Analytical leaders need to hire both data developers and analysts to run an effective analytics program. Data developers build data warehouses and complex reports and dashboards, while analysts explore data and answer ad hoc questions. Although there is cross-over among these roles, many analytics programs separate the positions of data developer and analyst. Of course, it's one thing to employ people with these skills, it's another to organize them into effective teams that consistently deliver business value. That's the subject of the next chapter.

CHAPTER 9

HOW DO YOU ORGANIZE DATA DEVELOPERS AND ANALYSTS?

Most new analytical leaders want to know how to organize an analytical team. Unfortunately, there is no tried-and-true formula; there are as many ways to organize analysts as there are companies to organize them. However, in talking with analytical leaders, most implement a federated organizational structure that encompasses both data developers and analysts. (See Chapter 8 for the difference between data developers and analysts.)

In a federated structure, analytical leaders centralize data developers within a corporate BI/DW team and maintain a loose affiliation with departmental data developers hired and supervised by department heads. Similarly, they maintain a corporate analysis team that consists of statisticians and a few business analysts who work on cross-functional projects and maintain a tight affiliation with embedded analysts who serve departmental needs.

DATA DEVELOPER TEAMS

Corporate data developers build the data warehouse, manage corporate metrics, and build cross-functional reports and dashboards, while departmental data developers build departmental reports and dashboards and local data marts, if needed. The corporate data development team (a.k.a. BI/DW team) usually resides in the IT department, but often works best when it's pulled out of IT—in full or part—and reports into a Chief Operating Officer or Chief Financial Officer. The departmental data developers usually report directly to the department head but sometimes to the director of analytics or head of the corporate BI/DW team.

In a well-run organization, both corporate and departmental data developers participate in a BI Center of Excellence that coordinates their activities. This federated group standardizes processes for managing projects, developing software, and defining data standards. They also select new tools and create a roadmap that guides development projects.

Unfortunately, many corporate BI/DW managers view departmental data developers as the "enemy", especially defacto data developers hired by the department head, not the director of analytics or head of the corporate BI/DW team. When left to their own devices, these sorts of departmental data developers often create an avalanche of spreadmarts and data shadow systems that undermine the work of the corporate BI/DW team.

However, savvy analytical managers identify and recruit these "renegade" data developers to serve as their "eyes and ears" within the Analytics Center of Excellence. This approach succeeds because departmental data developers often want and need a community to recognize and validate their work and share ideas and provide standards that simplify and speed development.

BOBI TEAMS

A few far-sighted companies implement business-oriented BI teams or BOBI. These BOBI teams overlay both corporate and departmental data development teams. The difference is that BOBI teams oversee the data strategy for the company and work closely with both corporate and departmental data developers. BOBI teams essentially split strategy from execution, leaving strategy in the business and execution in IT.

Specifically, BOBI teams develop the analytical roadmap, manage the budget, oversee data governance programs, and spearhead change management initiatives. They also gather business requirements and educate executives about the value of analytics and help them brainstorm new applications. They also manage metadata and develop standards for data, visualization, and end-user tools as well as track usage and manage end-user support and training. With a BOBI team in place, corporate data developers can focus on building the data warehouse and technical infrastructure rather than get bogged down interfacing with the business.

All of the analytical leaders profiled in this book, except Tim Leonard, run BOBI teams. (But Tim runs a very effective BI Center of Excellence, which he calls a BI Competency Center.) They often have the title of director of analytics, and they report to the CEO, COO, or CIO but never to the director of IT. These directors not only oversee a BOBI team, but all the other analytical teams discussed above, including the corporate BI/DW team, the corporate analyst team, all embedded analysts, statisticians, and database administrators, among other things.

Belichicking analytics. One reason our analytical leaders are effective at what they do is because they control both the analytical "front office" and "back office." In other words, they have end-to-end control over the analytical environment, which makes it easier to create synergies among different analytical teams. They are like the "Bill Belichick of analytics." When Belichick came to the New England Patriots in 2000, he not only took the position of head coach, but also the position of general manager of football operations, which gave him total control over the team, players, coaches, salaries, and recruiting. This level of authority was unprecedented at the time, but has helped Belichick become one of the most successful coaches in NFL history.

ANALYST TEAMS

Typically, organizations embed analysts (e.g. business analysts, statisticians, and data scientists) in each functional area so they can work closely with the business and gain the necessary knowledge to deliver effective insights.

As mentioned in Chapter 8, sometimes these analysts double as departmental report developers, making them "superusers" who are extensions of the corporate BI team. Some embedded analysts report to the director of analytics and have dotted line responsibility to the department head, while others report directly to department heads who set their daily priorities with dotted line responsibility to the director of analytics. It doesn't matter which approach an organization takes as long as the director of analytics communicates clearly with department heads so both departmental and enterprise analytical needs can be met.

Co-location. Analytical leaders profiled in the book wholeheartedly endorse the idea of co-locating business analysts and business users. Some, like Dan Ingle, use Scrum methods to bring analysts and business users in closer proximity, while others, including Ken Rudin, Kurt Thearling, and Eric Colson, advocate having analysts sit side by side with the business users they support. Whatever the technique, most believe that co-location is the key to quickly developing analytical solutions that meet business needs. For this reason, most refuse to hire business requirements analysts to serve as intermediaries between business users and BI developers or analysts.

Statisticians. The analytical leaders disagree when it comes to organizing statisticians and data scientists. Some believe it's important to centralize them in a collaborative community that fosters the exchange of ideas and knowledge, mentors new analysts, and provides a career path for veterans. Others believe it's important to embed statisticians into functional groups to keep them close to the business, just like business analysts. Large organizations with a sufficient number of statistical projects can afford to hire and embed statisticians in every department, but smaller organizations may not have this luxury.

In either case, it's important that statisticians belong to a central group which fosters knowledge sharing and establishes standards for managing data, developing models, and running projects. This central group, known as an Analytical Center of Excellence, oversees and manages all analysts, statisticians, and data scientists in a single organization that is managed by the direction of a director of analytics. In many cases, the Analytical Center of Excellence is an umbrella group that oversees all data warehousing, BI, and analytics initiatives and teams.

COMMENTARY OF ANALYTICAL LEADERS

RUDIN: When I was at Zynga, we had two groups of analysts. Analysts in the largest group were embedded in Zynga's game studios and used SQL and Tableau to analyze game data and create reports and dashboards for product managers. The other analysts worked in a central group and performed more complex analyses, such as correlating player behavior with desired outcomes. They used SQL and the "R" statistical package.

When I arrived at Zynga, all the analysts sat with me. We were what I call the "Analytical Priesthood." Game designers would come to us with questions and requests, and we would give them answers. I didn't like this flow. I thought it promoted the attitude among business people that analytics was something separate from what they do, and it put my team in a reactive mode. We had to wait for the business to ask questions. But often the questions they asked weren't that meaningful.

You can't create an analytics culture unless everyone is responsible for analytics, not just the analysts. In the same way, a manufacturing company can't improve quality until everyone takes responsibility for creating quality products. If you outsource quality to a single department, you give engineers and everybody else license not to worry about quality, since it's another group's responsibility. To get a quality product, everyone in the company has to think about quality.

EMBEDDED ANALYSTS. So, we decided to reverse the flow of traffic and embed our analysts in the game studios. This is the single biggest thing that we did as an analytics team to impact the company in a positive way. After that, the game designers didn't come to us, we came to them. We became part of their teams. Analysts now sit in the studios and hear what is going on. They get to know designers and participate in all their meetings. They develop a deep understanding of how the games work and what designers are trying to accomplish. And this allows them to gain credibility with designers, contribute to discussions, and help the studios achieve their goals.

For instance, one studio was trying to find ways to increase the number of players who purchased virtual goods. The analyst embedded in that studio shared the results of an analysis done by a colleague about the impact of embedding a charitable campaign into a game. The analyst told the designers that 30 percent of players who contributed to the charity inside a particular game had never purchased anything before, but half of them soon after made a second purchase. The analyst convinced the designers that adding such a feature would both raise millions for charity and prompt reluctant players to start playing the game. The designers bought into the idea and implemented it. And an analyst came up with that idea! That would never have happened if we had stuck with the priesthood model. Embedding analysts and making them part of the team makes them much more valuable. They dig deeper to solve problems.

CENTRAL COORDINATION. After I reorganized the team, only three analysts sat with me, and they worked on cross-functional projects. We moved all the other analysts to the studios, although they still technically reported to me. To maintain solidarity among our distributed team, we held a standup meeting for 15 minutes every morning to share ideas and knowledge. The team also met quarterly to set goals and review performance.

EXPERIMENTATION. Another key to embedding is making the analysts not just part of the team, but part of the process. And this is where experimentation became a critical asset. For example, designers might meet and discuss the pros and cons of two possible game features. A designer might say, "In my experience, we should do X and not Y." At that point, the analyst should raise his hand and say, "I appreciate your experience, but the reality is we don't really know the right answer. So let's test it." So the studio does an A/B test to determine which leads to the best results.

Through embedding, Zynga created a culture of experimentation. Designers don't think twice about implementing a new design feature without testing it. In fact, they get chewed out by the general manager of the studio or the president if they implement a major feature without first conducting an A/B experiment. So experimentation is now part of the process by which games evolve.

INGLE: Our statisticians sit with the business units, which fund their salaries, but they are also part of a central team. Business unit heads are responsible for reviewing statistical projects and contributing to the performance reviews of individual statisticians in their unit.

Embedding statisticians in business units gives statisticians a lot of gratification. This physical proximity enables them to answer a lot of questions quickly and deliver things the business never thought possible. Sitting in their cubicles, the statisticians often overhear business people ask questions that they never mention in meetings. In response, the statisticians will jump up like prairie dogs, and say, "I can get that for you." The business people usually have no idea the statisticians have that type of information. And when business unit heads walk outside their offices and see two statisticians pounding away on their problems, they know they're getting great value for their investment in analytics. Furthermore, they can bounce ideas off the statisticians and think through business problems in a way that normally doesn't happen in formal meetings.

We make sure that we assign statisticians to work with the right business counterparts. For instance, we assign less experienced statisticians to work with business stakeholders who have worked on analytical projects before and know what kinds of questions statistical models are designed to answer. Conversely, we pair business people with limited exposure to statistical models with our veteran statisticians who know how to translate analytics into the language of business.

CENTRAL TEAM. But our statisticians also belong to a central team, run by my colleague Shawn Hushman, which coordinates their work and enables them to share ideas and best practices. The central team has a daily standup meeting where members ask for suggestions about how to approach different types of statistical problems.

From a career perspective, a central group makes it easier for statisticians to find their niche, whether it's to continue as a statistician and move up the ranks, or switch to the product side and become a product manager. A central team also makes it easy for statisticians to periodically switch contexts and apply their knowledge to different part of the business, if they desire. This helps them cultivate their skills and stay challenged. A bored statistician doesn't stick around for long.

SCRUM FOR STATISTICIANS. A central group also makes it easier to standardize the way statisticians develop models and approach data. Shawn's team has taken a cue from us on the data side and now applies Scrum methods to developing analytical models. It's important that statisticians work closely with the data warehousing team to acquire, test, and validate data in the data warehouse so they can create their models.

For instance, Shawn's team works with my data acquisition team to define data acquisition rules and how data gets structured, and they help construct user acceptance tests. This partnership helps avoid turf wars and tribal knowledge that occurs when you have pockets of statisticians who manage their own data sets. More importantly, it saves statisticians considerable time since otherwise they'd have to source, clean, and integrate the data themselves.

So, we really have the best of both worlds. We gain productivity and insights by embedding our statisticians in business units, but we get cross-functional standards and coordination by managing them as a single unit. This hub-and-spoke approach raises everyone's analytical bar. Business stakeholders become more analytically savvy and proactive about using analytics to address certain types of problems and challenges. And, statisticians learn how to evaluate the relevance of their models from a business perspective, not just a statistical one.

 **THEARLING:** People often discuss whether it's better to distribute analysts throughout the organization or keep them centralized. I personally like a distributed model in which analysts are embedded in the business so they get to know the people, processes, and data. A central analytical team that takes orders doesn't work because it's too disconnected from the business. But, I do like central teams that offer guidance on the use of analytics in the organization. Rather than building analytical models, central teams develop best practices and procedures for how the models should be built. For instance, at Capital One, our chief scoring officer, Bill Kahn, created training and certification programs for in-house statisticians. He also created a governance processes for building and certifying models before putting them into production. I had a great partnership with Bill, and credit him with a great deal of success in moving our capabilities forward.

O'CONNOR: We have a hybrid model at Nokia for organizing analysts and data scientists. We have a centralized analytics team responsible for building the technology ecosystem, for collecting and managing the data asset, and for delivering some analytical insights into the overall health and applicability of that data asset. In parallel, we encourage every business unit to develop an analytical competency. Our central group is more focused on providing technology, managing the data asset, and partnering with distributed groups to help them exploit our data asset. In some cases, we might send a SWAT team to a business unit to work with them. But, ideally, they do the work themselves using our data and tools.

To build community, we have quarterly meetings where analysts share what they are doing in the field. At some of these meetings, people ask me, "What kind of analyses are you going to do for me?" And I say, "We are going to do analysis *with* you." In a sense, our centralized team is like the hub of a wheel. The hub contains the technology platform and analytical ecosystem that manage Nokia's data. The business units are like the spokes of the wheel. Each spoke conducts the analytical work in a particular subject matter. For example, our maps team mines our central data to determine how to provide the freshest, most up-to-date maps to consumers. Our search team crunches through terabytes of search logs and user-generated-content to improve search results. Our markets team uses phone activation logs and application usage logs to improve many business processes, including field inventory management and device readiness.

LEONARD: One of the first things I did when I came to U.S. Xpress was to recruit power users to work with our corporate BI team, which consists of report developers and data warehousing specialists. Our first task was to create an inventory of spreadmarts. When I arrived, we had hundreds of thousands of Excel spreadsheets and thousands of Access databases which people were using to make decisions. Power users created these data shadow systems because they couldn't rely on the IT team to deliver quality data quickly. So, I asked them to help create the inventory so they could see the scope of the problem and help address it. I also got the power users to help define consistent metrics and rules to use in our data warehouse, reports, and dashboards. Today, these power users are embedded in the business departments. They help create ad hoc reports for business colleagues and coordinate BI activities throughout the organization.

BICC. Recently, we created a BI Competency Center (BICC) to prioritize the development of analytical applications throughout the company. The BICC is run by a committee of business executives, along with me and our CIO. After our initial wins, we were so inundated with requests that I asked our CEO to create an executive committee within the BICC and assign his top lieutenants to it. Today, vice presidents from all major departments in the company sit on the committee, including Finance, Operations, and Sales. They meet every Friday for two to three hours to prioritize requests for new applications. In between meetings, they can review and approve smaller requests via a workflow tool. Essentially, this committee takes the political heat off my back and prioritizes projects that my team develops.

Thanks to one board member, we now have a litmus test for reviewing and approving such requests. We ask: 1) What is the business impact of this request? How will it help the company? 2) Who will use the application and how much? What metric do we use to determine usage? 3) Will it deliver business value in 90 days? Applying this litmus test reduced the number of spurious requests significantly. Now, it's almost a self-selecting process: only the serious candidates bother applying.

TAYLOR: Prior to 2004, the data warehouse at Blue KC was a shared responsibility between IT and the business, but that didn't work. In a matrixed environment, everybody and nobody was accountable for the outcome. Our data warehouse reflected this lack of leadership and accountability. It wasn't designed around subject areas, user adoption was low, and it didn't contain all the data the business needed. The data warehousing team also took a long time to deliver solutions because individual members had been enlisted to work on other projects and were only spending about half of their time on the data warehouse. That's what happens in a matrixed environment.

In 2003, we decided to relaunch the data warehouse. We knew the initiative wouldn't work if the data warehousing team reported to the IT department or any specific business unit. So I got put in charge and reported directly to the CIO instead of the head of IT. Our COO was the business sponsor.

We also knew that we had to build a business-technology team—not an

IT team or a business team. So, we pulled 15 analysts from the business and 15 technologists from the IT department, and put everyone in the right roles. We also brought in a consulting firm to help us put together a strategy and roadmap. We got approval for the strategy in late November, 2003, launched the project in January, 2004, and rolled out the first production version of the new data warehouse four months later, in May, 2004. Phew!

In late 2010, when we launched our analytical initiative, we took a similar approach, forming a dedicated team of five people, including an architect, two tool administrators, a trainer, and a director. We also contracted with an outside firm to build the data model for the analytical data mart and implement our analytical appliance, among other things. We also hired several statisticians on a freelance basis to build new propensity and risk models to augment the commercial models that we had purchased for the analytical solution.

COLSON: When designing an analytics organization, you need to create an enabling structure that allows you deliver value to business departments quickly and continuously, while maintaining cohesion. To do this, you need data development teams that are dedicated to individual departments and a central data platform team that builds and maintains the enterprise architecture to ensure cohesion and scale. And finally, you need an advanced analytics team with deep expertise in building analytical models.

DATA DEVELOPMENT TEAMS. Data developers should be dedicated to individual departments instead of being pooled into a central, shared service. This allows each department to set its own analytical agenda instead of fighting for resources with other departments. Although data developers report into a central analytics team, they have a dotted line relationship to departmental business heads, with whom they collaborate to set priorities.

The embedded developers do both analysis and development. Each data developer typically focuses on one subject area within the department they support, and works autonomously to deliver complete business solutions, including all data modeling, ETL development, and report writing, among other things. However, each coordinates with other data developers as needed to ensure their subject area models eventually align. I feel it's important to optimize what happens at the departmental level, even if it makes it harder to align across functional areas. This is a conscious decision.

It's important that embedded data developers sit side by side with the business people they support. This context gives them a better idea about what data to acquire and load into the data warehouse, and how to model data and build reports and dashboards that answer business questions. For example, they can pick up on non-verbal cues, such as the shrug of the shoulders, which a developer might read as, "Oh, that's something they don't care about." This type of context enables data to create great applications. Sometimes, data developers identify more with their departments than the analytics team, and that is not a bad thing. The key to our success is to be perfectly aligned with the business, not to function as a separate group.

. PLATFORM TEAM. The central data platform team develops and supports the enterprise architecture. This team focuses on technical context, not business context. It builds generic services available to all departments, such as database interfaces. The team saves developers from having to know the nuances of particular technologies and frees them to focus on business issues. The team also develops and supports the technical infrastructure, including storage and compute resources, such as Hadoop clusters. To be clear, embedded data developers don't have to coordinate their work with the platform team. They leverage the technical infrastructure that the platform team builds. The only people they coordinate with are other embedded data developers.

ADVANCED ANALYTICS. The advanced analytics team has a deep quantitative focus. They develop algorithms, conduct experiments, and do research to evolve the analytics methodology. Rather than embed them in the business, it's better to keep them together as a central group. Their work tends to be more project-oriented compared to the data developers who serve in a continuous support role. Furthermore, some departments don't have enough work to merit a full-time statistician. In addition, advanced analytics folks thrive in a more collegial environment where they can collaborate with peers, share quantitative techniques, and mentor newcomers.

SUMMARY

There are many ways to organize data developers and analysts. Although most data developers belong to a corporate BI/DW team that resides in the IT department, some work in business departments and are either formally or informally affiliated with the corporate BI/DW team or BI Center of Excellence. In terms of analysts, most companies embed them in business units and coordinate their activities through daily meetings and periodic offsite gatherings organized by the director of analytics or an Analytics Center of Excellence. And some companies, like Netflix, blend data developers and analysts into a single person who works in the business unit, yet reports to the corporate director of analytics.

However, even if an analytical team has the right people and organizational structure, it can still struggle if its data developers and analysts are not motivated. The next chapter discusses techniques for creating and maintaining high-performance analytical teams.

CHAPTER 10

HOW DO YOU MOTIVATE AND MANAGE DEVELOPERS AND ANALYSTS?

Effective analytical leaders know how to motivate and manage people on their teams. They are also strong leaders who are confident in their position and know when to delegate decisions.

Tim Leonard makes a great case for conducting bare-knuckles negotiations with executives about employee rewards and benefits before starting a program. Darren Taylor says it's important to align people's roles with their natural abilities and inclinations. Kurt Thearling explains that statisticians are a different breed of people who thrive in a collegial environment and continually seek new ways to hone their analytical skills. Dan Ingle emphasizes the importance of empowering teams, fostering teamwork and mutual trust, mentoring individuals and improving communications skills.

Finally, Ken Rudin makes a great distinction between leadership and management. Leaders focus on strategy, while managers focus on operations. The key to being a good leader, according to Rudin, is not to get sucked into being a manager. Good leaders teach employees to make their own operational decisions.

HIRING THE RIGHT PEOPLE

There have been thousands of books written and seminars delivered about how to motivate and manage people. In the context of analytics, perhaps the most important advice for analytical leaders is to hire the right people. Jim Collins, in his best-selling book "Good to Great", says great companies first get the right people "on the bus", and the wrong people off it, and then figure out where to drive it. Collins says that hiring good people with high emotional IQ and business sense is much more effective than hiring people based on skills and experience. That's because good people help define the strategy, while specialists become obsolete when the business strategy changes.

What this means for analytical leaders is that they shouldn't hire people just because they know a specific tool or programming language or have previous experience managing a specific task, such as quality assurance. If you need specialists, it sometimes may be better to outsource such positions to a low-cost provider or hire contractors. Top analytical leaders seek people who are ambitious, adaptable, and eager to learn new skills. Although analytical leaders should demand a certain level of technical competency and know-how, they ultimately want people who are passionate about data and working with business people to solve problems and achieve goals.

Collins adds that the right people "don't need to be tightly managed or fired up; they are self-motivated by an inner drive to produce the best results and be part of something great." In analytics, these people don't just show up to work and do a job; they want to put their stamp on the organization and make a difference. They work proactively to figure out the right things to do and then do them the right way. Unfortunately, these types of people are in short supply and you have to pay them more than the average worker. And you have to keep them challenged or they'll leave in a heartbeat. But they are worth the price.

Some analytical managers complain that they can't find these types of highly motivated and committed workers with decent technical and analytical skills. But if you can find one, you have a team. According to Eric Colson, that person is more effective than ten average workers and they feed off each other's energy and habits. If you are faced with hiring a "B" level person, sometimes it's better not to hire anyone at all. With "A" players, ana?lytical teams perform at a high level and are self perpetuating.

COMMENTARY FROM ANALYTICAL LEADERS

CREATE THE RIGHT INCENTIVES

LEONARD: I already mentioned the six week "death march" I put my team through at U.S. Xpress to get our first win. (See Chapter 7.) But that wouldn't have happened if I didn't first give the team encouragement and incentives. You need to know what they want—and it's not always money; sometimes it's recognition, training, and other things.

When I got to U.S. Xpress, the team was downtrodden and no one in the business believed they could do anything valuable for the company. The incentive I gave my team was not financial. I didn't promise them more money or training or tenure. I simply promised that if they delivered the project on time and under budget, they would be publicly recognized by the business. When we successfully completed the project, I got the sponsor to introduce each of my team members to the CFO, who recognized them for their work. That meant a lot to the team. And from that moment on, we stopped being an IT team and became a data delivery team.

When we picked up more projects, I negotiated more concrete terms with the CFO. I got the team an immediate pay increase and a training budget. That helped solidify their trust in me. They knew I would get them what I promised. The raises were based on achieving performance metrics. I doled out training on an ad hoc basis during projects to keep their morale and momentum going. I sent them to local courses and TDWI (The Data Warehousing Institute) conferences. We also brought in well-known experts for them to talk with.

It's really important to negotiate these benefits upfront with top executives. You have to be ready to walk away from the company if you don't get them.

You have to look into the executives' eyes and say, "If you can't give me a big reward pool for my team and the budget I need for the project, then I'm not the right person for the job." You have to be that committed. If not, they'll look at you and smell the weakness. I've walked away from a couple of places. For instance, one company gave me money and power, but nothing for my team, so I walked. Unless you can reward the team, you can't possibly succeed. You don't have to give them much, but it must be something they value.

Put People in the Right Roles

TAYLOR: It's important to get people into roles that align with their natural talents rather than groom them for jobs for which they aren't suited. This increases their productivity and satisfaction. We often use the Gallup Organization's *Strengths Finder* assessment tool as a baseline to help people understand their core strengths and personal styles.

For instance, at Blue KC, we had a developer who was an A+ player for more than 15 years. In 2004, we moved him from production support to a long-term strategic project, and his performance tanked. When we assessed his natural talents using the *Strengths Finder* tool, we discovered that he liked tactical work that allowed him to deliver quick fixes to operational problems. So, he was miserable working on a single, six-month strategic project, even though he, himself could not explain why. Although we thought we had given him a nice, high-profile opportunity, the change was a career death sentence for him! So, we moved him back to operational work, and he's a happy team member today, working as productively as ever.

CAREER PATHS. For years, our culture dictated that you worked your way up the ranks—from individual contributor to management—chasing a pay raise at each level. But when you take a top individual performer and make them a manager or put them in a role that doesn't fit the way they're naturally wired, they fail miserably. I've seen it dozens of times. As a result, we've created job families with greater salary and bonus potential for solo contributors who don't manage people, but who may be great technologists.

We also use the *Strengths Finder* tool, when possible, to create our project teams. We map people's talents to the nature of the project. If it's a two-year, strategic project, we look for people who exhibit the "strategic" characteristic in the *Strengths Finder* assessment. That's the type of person you want to set the direction, vision, and architecture. Once the design work is done, you reassign that person to another strategic project, and replace them with more operationally minded people.

MOTIVATING STATISTICIANS

 **THEARLING:** At Capital One, we had a large community of statisticians. Some were veterans with many years of experience while others were fresh out of college. What was critical was the sense of community that was created among the statisticians. When we brought people right out of college, we would put them through an apprenticeship program to acclimate them to our data and analytics environment. We would assign new hires to projects and pair them with experienced statisticians.

For veteran statisticians, we provided certification and ongoing education. For instance, we held a semi-annual meeting of statisticians. At this event, individual statisticians would deliver presentations about new techniques or approaches to solving particular problems or lessons learned from mistakes they made. There were also sessions about our internal certification process and other administrative topics. We also brought in external speakers.

Statisticians like new challenges, so it's important to give them opportunities to apply analytics to new business domains. Unfortunately, this rarely happens in most organizations. Department heads are content to have good statisticians do the same things forever, but this isn't healthy. For many, the only way to tackle new challenges is to switch companies. Many analysts do this, but it doesn't have to be that way. A well-run company gives statisticians the opportunity to move between departments so they can tackle different problems. Or, they'll give them an alternative career path in which they can work towards becoming a manager or scoring officer.

We also taught statistics to business analysts. We didn't expect them to build production ready models; we just wanted them have a background in statistics so they could communicate more effectively with our statisticians. It worked.

 **INGLE:** As a leader, my approach is to be transparent and open. This engenders trust, both from above and below. For instance, I meet with my CEO every month and give him the good and bad news. I don't hide the bad news from him. I explain why we had a failure and what it cost us. Perhaps we ran a sprint that didn't work, or we underestimated the difficulty of meeting some requirements. I also ask the CEO to participate in our sprint review meetings so he can see what we're building and how we do it.

EMPOWER TEAMS. One important way to motivate teams is to empower them, not dictate what they do. Teams deliver better solutions in shorter time frames if you allow them to exercise their own judgment. The key is to hire the right people, train them, point them in the right direction and get out of the way. Give them a flexible framework, like Scrum, to follow. Although Scrum has a few non-negotiable elements, it is not a step-by-step playbook. (See Chapter 11.) Scrum gives teams a lot of freedom. This is especially important with today's workers, who expect a higher degree of autonomy than workers did even a generation ago. It is a rare day when the "my way or the highway" approach to managing a team gets good results.

FOCUS ON TEAMWORK

We spend a lot of time at Kelley Blue Book fostering teamwork. I make everyone who joins my team read the book, *The Five Dysfunctions of a Team* by Patrick Lencioni. He lays out a simple model that explains what makes an effective team. We talk about the concepts in the book as a team, and then do follow-on exercises to improve our teamwork. Our human resources department has even built a curriculum around the book. It is common to hear people referring to the "5 D's" when you walk the floors and conference rooms in our office. The terms have become part of our corporate jargon.

Lencioni says that the foundation of a good team is trust. Without trust, team members don't risk saying what they think, and this results in a lack of healthy debate, which is critical to generating great solutions. If a person thinks they're going to get blasted for voicing an opinion, they don't. Instead, they take a passive-aggressive approach that tries to manipulate the situation in their favor. But, when people feel safe to express their ideas, the team can explore a lot of options in a short period of time, refine the most promising ones, and build consensus around one. This approach always results in a better solution that all team members can stand behind.

VOLUNTARY 360-DEGREE REVIEWS. One of the more powerful exercises we do is a group-based 360-degree review. We bring the team together around a table. Each person has to write down the strengths, weaknesses, and opportunities of each person on the team and then share what they wrote with the rest of the group. That's terrifying, not only for the person giving the critique, but also for the person receiving it. But it breaks down barriers, clears the air and binds people closer together. The process builds trust and tolerance, creates accountability and gets people comfortable with being vulnerable.

This commitment to teamwork aligns perfectly with Scrum development techniques because Scrum is all about team. Scrum teams are self-organizing. They consist of developers, architects, testers, users, and product owners. Individuals must commit to the team and each other. They succeed or fail together as a team, not a collection of individuals. You never hear a team member say, "Well, I did my part." At the beginning of a sprint, the team identifies the tasks required to complete each story [i.e., business require-ments] and estimates the time for each task. Then, as a team, they commit to delivering a certain number of stories per sprint, and the entire team is held accountable for the outcome.

At the end of each three-week sprint, the team holds a review session in which they present what they created to the project owners, but anyone in the company can attend as well, from the CEO on down. The team steps through what it created during the previous sprint and often delivers a demo. If the team didn't finish the sprint, they have to explain why. Knowing that the CEO might attend your sprint review meeting motivates everyone to do their best!

ESTABLISH A MENTORING PROGRAM

In doing succession planning recently with my management team, I recognized that we needed to improve the leadership skills of people within our division. Now, we developed a mentoring program to cultivate our next generation of analytical leaders. So, now we identify individual contributors with leadership potential and put them in a mentorship program. We assign them to a manager from a different department who works with them on a one-on-one basis over an extended period of time. The goal is to help these aspiring leaders to identify skills they need to achieve their career goals.

I currently mentor five people in the organization. During the initial meeting, I ask the individuals to identify ten characteristics of an effective leader based on people they know and admire. I then get each person's peers to give them a 360-degree review based on those leadership traits. From that feedback, we identify a few skills and traits that they might want to improve and that becomes the focal point of our regular discussions. From that point, it's up to them to do the heavy lifting and make the changes they need to become a better leader. For instance, one person whom I mentor perceives himself as a well-liked, non-confrontational manager who goes with the flow. But the feedback from his peers suggested he was too soft, and they wanted him to provide more direction and take charge. So, I'm working with him to become more decisive.

FOSTER GOOD COMMUNICATION

I also encourage people to get visual in meetings. I ask them to draw on a white-board instead of talking about something in the abstract. I encourage them to give real-life examples when they are trying to explain data structures or statistical models. I'm amazed at the number of times people talk in a meeting without communicating. One person says something and another thinks they get it, but I can tell they don't. This is endemic when business people and IT professionals converse.

As a result, I encourage people to ask questions when they are uncertain about something and not worry about being judged. I tell people that if you aren't clear about something, other people in room probably feel the same way. There are no dumb questions. The subjects that we discuss in analytics are not simple; some of it is pretty challenging. When you combine complex business processes with sophisticated technologies, you can't possibly know everything. So, I tell people that it's o.k. to ask "dumb" questions and admit you don't understand something. Usually, everyone else has the question you do!

LEAD, DON'T MANAGE

 **RUDIN:** I try to delegate as much as possible to my team. I want them to do more of what I'm doing so I can do other things. When a problem arises and someone asks me what we should do about it, my standard response is, "I don't know. What do you think?" If they have an issue, I discuss it with them, but I'll let them make the decision.

I used to think that as a manager, I should have all the answers. But people know their jobs better than I do. It's a mistake when a manager becomes the ultimate decision maker for everything. That's a quick way to become a bottleneck. When staff members have a question, I push back and ask them to answer their own question. This is how they develop problem solving skills. By exercising their own judgment, intuition, and creativity, they gain confidence solving problems. And it frees my time, as well.

My job is to set overall goals for my teams and clear away all the roadblocks so they can focus on doing their jobs. My job is to think strategically, not manage operations. To me, there's a big difference between management and leadership. Both are necessary, but they're different. Management is about keeping the trains running on time and fixing broken tracks. It's about making sure you stick to your plan. In essence, management is about making sure things don't change. I let my team handle management tasks.

Leadership, however, is all about change. Leaders ask, "What do we need to change today to be better tomorrow? What processes need to change? What new opportunities do we need to exploit? I spend most of my time focusing on what we need to do differently and how to make those changes happen. In reality, I and my team both do some management and some leadership, but I try to give my team most of the management responsibilities.

SUMMARY

Creating a strong, talented, and motivated analytical team is critical to success. The key is to hire the right people, put them in the right jobs, obtain the right incentives, foster teamwork and self-awareness, and know when to lead and when to manage. With the right team in place, the next step is to implement processes that ensure the timely delivery of analytical solutions. Uncovering the secrets of agile development is the focus of the next chapter.

CHAPTER 11

HOW DO YOU SPEED TIME TO DELIVERY?

THE PRINCIPLE OF PROXIMITY

Several years ago, after talking with a number of analytical leaders, I discovered the secret to developing successful data applications fast: the principle of proximity. That is, to deliver great applications, seat your data developers alongside your business users. Not just in a joint-application design session, a requirements interview, or Scrum stand-up, but all the time! The idea behind the principle of proximity is to make developers and business users work side by side, elbow to elbow, nose to nose. You don't merely locate them on the same campus or in the same building; you put them in the same cubicle block, or better yet, in one big room with no walls, so everyone can see, hear, and touch everyone else all the time. It's radical, but effective.

And don't be mistaken, I'm not talking about business requirements analysts—I'm talking about data developers who write the ETL code, statisticians who design the models, and report writers who create dashboards and reports. The idea is to make data developers get the requirements directly from business users instead of second hand through a business requirements analyst where something always gets lost in translation.

In essence, to develop great analytical applications fast, you have to function like a small startup, where there are no departments, teams, or organizational boundaries; no separate jargon and incentives; no separate managers and objectives; and no walls. Just one big, messy, energetic, on-the-same-wavelength team that gets things done. And fast.

AGILE METHODOLOGIES

I like agile software development methods. They come as close as any methodology to approximating the principle of proximity. If nothing else, go agile. Create a small team of business and technical people and make them do stand-up meetings daily. Require business users to write requirements as "stories" on 3x5 index cards; make developers deliver working features in two to four week sprints; allow users to "reshuffle" their story cards after a sprint; hold the team jointly accountable for the outcome; and make them review their output and processes with business users at the end of every sprint.

This is what Dan Ingle of Kelley Blue Book advocates, and it works great. He says Scrum works best with strong teams that are willing to succeed or fail together. To create this atmosphere, Ingle fosters teamwork and trust among team members, as we learned in the last chapter. This is the cornerstone of healthy Scrum teams.

Common Sense versus Ideology. According to Ken Collier in his book *Agile Analytics: A Value-driven Approach to Business Intelligence and Data Warehousing*, agile BI methods value:

- *Individuals and interactions over processes and tools*
- *Working BI systems over comprehensive documentation*
- *End user and stakeholder collaboration over contract negotiation*
- *Responding to change over following a plan*

These core principles of agile development represent the triumph of common sense over rigid ideology. They account for change, negotiation, and the messiness of the human condition. (Although some in the agile world exhibit another human tendency, which is to totemize artifacts. These purists turn Scrum into a rigid methodology and they ostracize anyone who violates any tenets of the code.)

Applied to data. Although agile methods were invented to improve the development of transaction processing applications, most analytical practitioners have figured out how to apply the methods to analytical applications and data infrastructures. To accommodate architectural requirements, analytical practitioners generally extend the length of sprints when sourcing new data and periodically devote a sprint or two to refactoring code and realigning subject-area data models.

But as good as agile can be, proximity is better. Why? When you place developers and business experts in the same room, they almost don't need to talk. They absorb what they need to know almost by osmosis, and they learn to respect each other and the work they do. And fewer meetings make happier, more productive people. Not surprisingly, Dan Ingle, a big Scrum champion, also advocates co-location (his term for the principle of proximity.) In fact, Ingle says that some business analysts at Kelley Blue Book spend upwards of 80% of their time sitting with data developers.

Spanners. Eric Colson goes one step further than agile. Colson has always worked at fast-paced internet companies where rapid change is constant. So, he created a development methodology that is faster than agile. He introduced the notion of a "spanner"—a data developer who builds an entire analytical application singlehandedly. The person "spans" all the functions required to build a data solution, from requirements to modeling to testing. Colson claims that one spanner works faster than a team of specialists, because a spanner doesn't have to wait for others to complete tasks. And they produce better results since they have the business context to know what users want and the autonomy to discover requirements as they go along.

COMMENTARY FROM ANALYTICAL LEADERS

 **INGLE:** About 12 years ago, there were many horror stories out there of people struggling to build gigantic data warehouses using a big bang approach. I didn't want to go down that path, so I started designing data warehouses incrementally and iteratively, developing one business subject area at a time.

My team didn't follow any specific published methodology; we simply did what made sense. We'd go from requirements to a working prototype in a matter of weeks, and we didn't flesh out every attribute in every dimension. The point was to build something quickly to show users, get their feedback, rearrange facts and dimensions, and refactor ETL code as needed. We wanted to be transparent and open about what we did. We wanted to fail fast so that within two weeks we'd know whether we were headed down the right track or not.

ADOPTING SCRUM

Looking back, we followed a lot of tenets of the Scrum methodology without knowing it. For instance, we worked in small teams of co-located business and technical people, and we ran short, fixed duration cycles. We didn't formalize the Scrum methodology until about 2003. The formal methodology helped us scale our development efforts and provide consistency across teams. That was important because my group grew to more than 100 people and multiple teams spanning several different technology disciplines.

When I came to Kelley Blue Book in 2006, someone showed me a set of old metal shelves crammed with large three-ring binders full of requirements from three prior attempts to replace a key legacy system. In my mind, I was thinking, "What is the definition of insanity? Doing the same thing over again and expecting a different result." Those three-ring binders were a symbolic reminder why those projects didn't succeed.

Learn from failure. Before I came to Kelley Blue Book, the technology team had attempted to migrate from a Waterfall to Scrum development methodology. The result resembled something closer to "scrumerfall"—the teams used

Scrum terminology and artifacts, but still followed traditional analysis, design, construction and implementation phases. As a leadership team, we convinced the organization to re-commit to using Scrum and provided additional training and coaching. We also educated executives about the concepts of agile development, and they bought into the methodology, giving the approach their full support.

To get things going, I served as Scrum Master for one of the teams. My first Scrum team struggled at various points and that spooked my boss. He came to me and said, "What are you going to do about this?" I said with a smile, "Nothing!"

The best thing you can do for a Scrum team is allow it to fail. It's hard to watch, for sure. But failure usually brings a team closer together, and the members learn from their mistakes. If you prop them up, you deny them the opportunity to make a big leap in productivity and cohesiveness. That Scrum team that we allowed to fail is now arguably the most effective team in the company.

If a Scrum team fails, you only lose a few weeks. Obviously as a leader, you need to weigh the risks before letting a team fail. If the stakes are too high, you need to protect the company first. In a long term project, however, a few weeks doesn't make or break a project.

KEYS TO SUCCESS

BUILD TRUST. There are many key ingredients to making Scrum work, but building trust among team members is the biggest. We spend considerable time at Kelley Blue Book building trust. (See Ingle's commentary in Chapter 9.) Trust doesn't naturally bloom in the workplace. We aren't necessarily taught to behave in that way in corporate America. People are afraid to show weakness for fear it might be used against them later. As a result, people never learn how to rely on others and work as an effective team. In our Scrum process, managers don't tell people to do A, B and C. Team members select their own tasks for each sprint, but work together to fulfill commitments made collectively by the team. They need to adopt the mantra, "We are going to fail or succeed as a team."

RETROSPECTIVES. We don't skewer people or teams for making mistakes. We seek to learn from mistakes and not repeat them again. At the end of every sprint, each team does a retrospective in which members discuss what worked, what didn't, and what they can do differently in the next sprint. Since our sprints are normally three week cycles, teams constantly assess their processes and performance. This is critical to success.

PROXIMITY. Co-location is also a critical ingredient in the success of our Scrum process. When we launch a project, the first step is to identify the team members and carve out the necessary office space for the entire group to work in close proximity. We will often move people upstairs or downstairs in our building for the duration of a project. That way, for instance, Bob can turn his chair around and say, "Hey, Sharon, what did you mean when you said this? I'm looking at the source data. Is this what you were thinking?" And everyone else in the vicinity can hear the conversation, which is important, since we don't force the teams to create reams of documentation. This is much more efficient than waiting for a biweekly meeting to ask questions and clarify requirements.

The interesting thing is that the analysts enjoy sitting upstairs with our data warehousing team. It gives them a break from assessing the value of vehicles all day. They also know the project will benefit them, so they have a vested interest in shaping the outcome. They also gain technical knowledge, which makes them a more educated and effective business partner.

For instance, by working daily with our developers, analysts begin to understand the scope of their requests, whether they are monumental or incremental. They also learn that the data team needs to pause once in a while to reset its architecture and work through "technical debt," which involves rewriting code to align early iterations with subsequent development. Ultimately, we try to make business people more conversant with the technology so they are a more educated consumer who participates in the process. And we try to make technology people more conversant in the business by having them interact constantly with business people.

TEAM SIZE. The size of a Scrum team also factors into its success. For example, one of our Scrum teams expanded to more than 20 people to meet business demand. However, once the team grew past 12 members, we began to notice that it had difficulty communicating, and it fell short in some key metrics that we track for each sprint. So, we decided to split that large team into two smaller teams and gave each a different data domain. This change has yielded solid results, increasing the effectiveness and efficiency of both groups.

SELLING SCRUM

It's important to roll out Scrum to everybody, including executives, department heads, analysts, and developers. You have to give executives full disclosure about what is happening, failures and all. The Scrum process is not roses and champagne. Some tasks are difficult to accomplish incrementally, like building a data warehousing architecture. You need to account for rework and refactoring, which some executives think is wasteful. But you have to convince them that the benefit of getting a solution faster and learning what works and doesn't early in the process outweighs any refactoring costs.

Department heads, analysts, and developers also need to buy into the process. If department heads don't let their people participate on a daily basis and sit with our technology teams, Scrum wasn't going to work. You have to teach business analysts, product managers, and developers how to work in a Scrum team and make sure they don't revert to more traditional approaches. This is another reason I served as a Scrum Master, to stay close to the action and keep people on track until the process became baked into their work habits.

DATA ACQUISITION

Many of our Scrum efforts today focus on data acquisition, either acquiring new data sources or managing changes to existing ones. For instance, one of our major providers of auction data recently changed its data feed, giving us more granular data. So the data analysts on that data acquisition team worked with statisticians to generate a series of stories related to the changes. The data analysts defined what the new data elements would mean, while the statisticians assessed the value of those elements for their statistical models. Both participated in user acceptance testing as part of the Scrum process and verified that the new data acquisition jobs delivered the proper data.

KANBAN. We are now exploring an alternative development method known as Kanban, to further accelerate our data acquisition process, among other things. Kanban is a framework for scheduling just-in-time deliveries in a manufacturing environment. For us, this means that instead of planning a three-week sprint, we'll create a work queue based on the team's capacity and stream tasks through the queue. The goal is to focus on the velocity of work not a fixed set of deliverables. When the team finishes one task, it immediately tackles the next highest priority item in the queue and swarms it with resources to get it done as quickly as possible. I think this approach could help us adapt more quickly to changing priorities in the data acquisition space as well as in the creation of dashboards and reports.

COLSON: To move quickly, you need to make your data developers as autonomous as possible. Dependence on functional specialists is one of the primary reasons why many companies struggle to deliver data solutions quickly.

To build an end-to-end data solution, a development team must gather requirements, analyze source systems, create data models, build ETL programs, develop report objects, create reports and dashboards, and test the output. Traditional development shops hire specialists to handle each of these functions. This strategy emerged out of the industrial era as a way to increase the efficiency of building non-differentiated products for a mass market. But data solutions are highly customized and requirements continually change. In fact, requirements only crystallize as you iterate through the development process. So, it doesn't make sense to use an assembly line approach and technical specialists to build data solutions.

COORDINATION COSTS. The major challenge with technical specialists is that you need a lot of them to deliver a complete solution. The cost of coordinating specialists, who are normally assigned to multiple, concurrent projects, dwarfs the value they offer. Specialists might only need two hours to perform a particular task, but if they're not available for two weeks, then it takes them two weeks to complete the two-hour task! That is, the wait-time to perform a task is materially greater than the actual work-time required. This won't help you deliver faster. But this is how most companies approach data development. They assign more developers to a project rather than fewer, and this increases the time required to deliver a data solution rather than shortens it.

THE SPANNER

Agile data teams flip this dynamic and assign as few developers as possible to each project. In fact, I believe the best approach is to assign a single developer with a diverse set of skills to a narrow business domain—say a single subject area. I call these people "spanners" because their skills and project scope "span" the entire business intelligence (BI) stack, including requirements, data sourcing, data modeling, ETL development, report writing, and testing. Spanners work much faster and more effectively than teams of specialists because they don't have to wait for others to complete tasks or attend meetings to explain changes in requirements and coordinate development.

BROADER PERSPECTIVE. Spanners also build better solutions because they have a broader perspective and more business context than specialists who only see and touch a part of the solution. For example, a report developer might build a hierarchy in a reporting tool, whereas a spanner will embed the hierarchy in the data layer to optimize performance and facilitate broader data access. The report developer doesn't own or work on the data model, so he doesn't consider making changes there, and as a result, delivers a sub-optimal solution. But a spanner will implement the hierarchy in the right place because he controls all elements of the BI stack and sees the big picture.

BUSINESS CONTEXT. Spanners also know the full context of a project and all its nuances, which enables them to make quick judgments and work faster. For example, spanners knows the source data, how it was transformed, the shape and value of the data, and all the business rules that govern it. When spanners see a weird number in a report, they don't have to ask the ETL guy what's going on since they already know the lineage of the data. As a result, they can spot problems others may not notice. They can also write their own tests since they know the application and data better than any quality assurance specialist.

Spanners also learn new things as they go along and incorporate this knowledge into the next project iteration. Since they continually work with the same business people on the same subject area, they aren't bound by a requirements document created by someone else. They feel free to make course corrections and break "the rules" when that's the right thing to do for the business. They often contribute ideas to make the solution better, rather than simply take orders. For example, a spanner might say to a business user, "The source data isn't organized the way you want to see the data, but if we combine it with external data from Twitter and Facebook, you'll get what you want." And the user replies, "Yes, that's exactly what I want."

In other words, spanners form partnerships with the business to build solutions. Spanners deliver technical knowledge and skills, while business people contribute domain knowledge and skills. Melding the two creates better data solutions.

MOTIVATION

In addition to delivering both faster and better solutions, spanners are more motivated than specialists because they own the entire project and take the full credit or blame. They have greater autonomy and are not dependent on others for success. They are completely accountable for the outcomes and cannot point fingers at others for slipped deadlines or bugs. As a result, spanners are passionate, dedicated, and highly productive.

According to Dan Pink, author of *Drive*, people derive job satisfaction from three things: autonomy, mastery, and purpose. Spanners enjoy all three. They have autonomy because they own and produce complete solutions. They control the design and can move as fast as they want. I can't tell you how often I hear colleagues in other companies gripe because they have to wait for ETL resources to become available or database performance is slow because "the DBA got the physical structures wrong." The spanner has full control over these things and the ability to make all necessary changes.

In addition, spanners have mastery because they know a business subject area inside and out and take pride in their stewardship. They often volunteer to give internal talks about their subject area and mentor new hires about how to use the data. Last, they have purpose because they clearly can see how their contributions impact the business, and they celebrate wins with the business teams they support.

SPANNER DOWNSIDES. There are downsides to the spanner approach. Not every developer has the skills to become a spanner, nor wants to be one. Spanners command a higher salary than regular developers and you have to buy a lot more software licenses to ensure spanners have all the tools they need. And some organizations are just too top-down driven or immersed in an assembly line approach for spanning to take root. As a result, you typically see spanners in fast-moving internet companies or startups.

O'CONNOR: We speed delivery in two ways – for the overall business, it's imperative that my central analytics team proactively collects and manages data prior to when business teams ask for it. And we have to make quality data available to the appropriate business teams via the best tools when they need it. This allows the business teams to focus on getting their job done – whether it's providing better music recommendations, more accurate maps, more efficient channel inventory management, or other things. Being proactive enables the business to come up with new product ideas and get those ideas to market quickly.

The second thing we do is to apply agile techniques to deliver data to the rest of the business. We have an interesting approach to agile development because we cherry pick the tools and techniques we use. For instance, we use two week sprints to focus our development and sprint exits to explain what worked and – just as importantly – what didn't work. Daily standups help us to quickly find and address impediments. One thing our agile teams don't do is simply pick tasks from a backlog for each sprint. We have specialists on certain datasets and ETL processes so we carefully plan each sprint to ensure we align the highest priority work with the best resources for that work.

SUMMARY

When it comes to building reports, dashboards, and data warehouses, organizations need to use every trick in the book to deliver solutions quickly that delight customers. The old waterfall method, which is based on an assembly line approach to software development, injects too much overhead and specialization into the process, slowing development to a crawl, increasing costs, and undermining user satisfaction. The key to accelerating development is to co-locate developers and business users so they function as a single team. Whether that is done through agile techniques like Scrum or spanners depends on the culture of the organization.

Analytical solutions are needed to deliver business insights. But as Ken Rudin asserts in the next chapter, insights are not the goal of analytics. The goal is actions that impact the business in a positive way.

CHAPTER 12

HOW DO YOU DELIVER INSIGHTS THAT MATTER?

Many experts believe the holy grail of analytics is to deliver "actionable insights." Ken Rudin disagrees. He argues that the goal of analytics is to improve the business. In other words, it's not the insights that count; it's the impact. He claims that insights without impact are useless.

Similarly, Rudin argues that analysts shouldn't focus on getting the right answers, they should focus on asking the right questions. Many questions that analysts ask simply aren't worth exploring because the answers aren't actionable. In other words, brilliant insights that the business can't use and act on are a waste of time. Rather, analysts need to ask questions whose answers drive key metrics of performance.

TESTING ASSUMPTIONS

Analytics is a testing ground for new ideas. It's a testbed for hypotheses. As Rudin explains, we need to get better at creating testable hypotheses, rather than seeking answers to questions that don't help the business.

One way to test hypotheses is to create analytical models. Every executive has assumptions—whether conscious or not—about what drives customer behavior or business activity. Often, these are million dollar assumptions that go unchallenged and untested, potentially costing companies a pretty penny if they are wrong, and they usually are. The modeling process encourages business people to surface and articulate these assumptions and submit them for testing before acting on them.

Hypothesis proved wrong. For example, a marketing executive at an online supplier of office supplies believed that customers located within one square mile of a competitor's physical store were more likely to churn than those located further away. Since the company only sold office supplies online, this was a reasonable assumption. Fortunately, the marketing director was savvy enough to bring his hypothesis to the analytical team before baking it into an expensive marketing campaign. Using historical data and an analytical workbench, the team disproved the hypothesis: they discovered that there was no correlation between a customer's likelihood to churn and their proximity to a big box-store competitor. This saved the company millions of dollars on a marketing campaign that would not have generated any measureable lift.

Analytics has a simple workflow: data to insights to action. However, the ultimate goal of analytics is a positive impact on the business, but too often, we focus our attention only on the data or the insights, or even the action. We often lose sight of the goal because corralling data and generating insights require an enormous amount of time, money, and technology. But Ken Rudin reminds us that it pays to stay focused on impacts, not insights. This chapter is devoted to Rudin's perspective on analytics and how to stay focused on what really counts.

COMMENTARY OF ANALYTICAL LEADERS

FOCUS ON QUESTIONS, NOT ANSWERS

 **RUDIN:** One important key to analytical success is to focus on questions, not answers. Most technologists fail to meet business needs because they focus on getting the right answers, not asking the right questions. But getting answers is easy. Tons of tools are available today to help a reasonably smart person find the answer to nearly any question. Given that getting answers has become easy, the real value comes from getting the business to ask the right questions first.

For instance, a key driver of profitability at Zynga is player longevity. That is, the longer someone plays an online game, the more money they are likely spend on virtual goods, which are non-physical objects, such as seed, swords, or tools that players can buy in the games. (Zynga makes money primarily by selling virtual goods, not through advertising or subscriptions.) Thus, a key objective for game designers is to create games that increase player engagement and longevity in the games.

When I arrived at Zynga three years ago, most of the company's game designers shared an assumption about what drives player longevity. They believed that the number of "neighbors" a player has correlates with time people spend playing the game. (Neighbors are friends with whom you play online games.) The more neighbors a player has, the more they play and the more virtual goods they buy. Or so they thought.

At one point I realized that we had never really tested that assumption. So we ran the numbers and discovered that there was no correlation between the number of neighbors and the time a player spends playing the game. This was a bit of a shock, because it was a core belief among designers. But we did discover another correlation. It's not the *number* of neighbors a player has that drives longevity, it's the *degree of engagement* with their neighbors that determines how long a player stays in the game.

That realization, which the game designers eventually bought into, changed the way they designed the games. For instance, in Farmville, if you want a barn to house your animals, you need to enlist your neighbors to help you build the barn because it's difficult to build it yourself. Fostering player-to-player engagement has increased Zynga's revenues. This shows that you can use analytics to drive key business operations.

Another example is what we do with our engagement metric, which is a measure of how frequently users play our games. The temptation is to simply measure the degree of engagement and show how it's trending. But that metric doesn't do much for the business. The real question is what you do about it. So, we realized that we shouldn't focus on what our engagement levels are, but rather the things that *drive* engagement. The question is more important than the answers. If a game designer asks us about engagement levels, we don't simply give them the answer; we ask them what drives engagement. That adds more value.

LUCIDERA. I learned the hard way about the importance of focusing on questions rather than answers at LucidEra, the company I started that sold cloud-based business intelligence (BI) tools and applications. Our goal was to make it easy for people to get answers to business questions and I think we did a good job of that. But we found that usage trailed off shortly after they subscribed to the service. This was frustrating because the tool was easy to use and enabled people to answer sophisticated analytical questions. There was nothing to install and it was easy to generate reports.

When we investigated this issue with our customers, we discovered they used our tool to generate the same reports they had built in Excel. Sure, our reports were automatically refreshed, looked a little nicer, and were more inter-active, but at end of day, they weren't getting any additional value from our tool. So, many of our customers went right back to using their Excel reports.

Often, our customers told us that they couldn't recreate the analysis process that our presales folks had demonstrated during the initial sales call. And that's when I realized that although we had given them a tool to provide really easy answers, they didn't know what questions to ask. By default, they asked the same questions they always did. And if you ask the same questions, you always get the same answers. So, the tool did nothing to improve their business performance.

So, we then switched to selling pre-built, value-added reports that addressed the questions they never thought to ask before. We pivoted our focus from delivering a tool to delivering applications, such as our "Pipeline Health Check", which helped sales executives ask the right questions to analyze the quality of their sales pipelines. They loved it.

For example, most sales organizations look at their sales cycle, which is how long it takes to win a deal. If your sales cycle is getting longer, then you might do more sales training or create better collateral to shorten the sales cycle, but these only make incremental improvements. Rather than asking how long it takes to win a deal, it's equally important and often more actionable to look at how long it takes to lose deals.

Say you discover that on average, you win deals in 90 days, but spend 250 days on deals that you lose. (By the way, sales reps usually spend more time on the deals they lose than deals they win.) As a next step, you plot the win rate on a graph, and you discover that once a deal exceeds 180 days in the pipeline, the close rate drops from 30% to 5%. The conclusion is obvious: if a deal takes longer than 180 days to close, you rarely win them.

Executives love this type of analysis because they can take immediate action. They can shut down all deals exceeding 180 days and instruct the sales people to call the customers and say, "Hey, it looks like it's not the right time for you to buy from us. We'll reengage with you next year."

So, if you focus on the right questions, you can directly affect business performance.

FOCUS ON IMPACTS, NOT INSIGHTS

The goal of the analytical team at Zynga is to change behavior, not deliver insights. I don't care if an insight is clever or the math is brilliant, if it doesn't produce results or change anything for the better, it adds no value. The goal is not to produce actionable insights; the goal is to produce results. Insights are a requirement, not a goal. An actionable insight that no one acts on is worthless. If people don't act on insights, then there's no point in hiring analysts. The company would do better by saving everyone's salaries than paying people to generate reports and insights that have no impact on the business.

As a former software marketer, I think of insights as products. As a marketer, your goal is to get people to buy and adopt your products. To do this, you first have to figure out what products to build. So you do market research, talk to people, and figure out what they want and need. What you don't do is build a product and then figure out who might want it.

You have to get creative when focusing on impacts instead of insights. This comes back to asking the right questions. Sometimes you have to wrestle with what really drives performance. If you can't come up with anything, then maybe the project isn't worth doing because you can't influence the outcome. Focusing on impacts instead of insights is great discipline. It focuses the team with laser intensity on business needs and makes it easier to prioritize what to analyze.

At Zynga, I asked our analysts to find out the biggest headaches facing the studios. Are they struggling to grow daily users? Reduce churn? Or monetize user engagements? Or perhaps they want to grow their international footprint or the number of mobile users. Or maybe they want to know how many resources to allocate to social networks in China versus South America.

For instance, if a studio says its biggest objective is to grow internationally by 10 percent, we adopt that metric as our own. In other words, the analysts share the same goals and metrics as the studios. We are part of the same team, working together to achieve a common goal. So we should be measured the same way. That just makes sense.

We avoid delivering insights that the studios aren't interested in. For instance, we could tell them we've discovered a way to detect fraud in half the time, which certainly has some value. But if they have other priorities and won't adopt it, we wasted our time developing the fraud model. So, by focusing on business needs, we prioritize our work and focus on insights that the studios want and will act on. We don't always succeed, but this process improves the odds of delivering insights that impact the business.

MEASURING IMPACTS

At Zynga, we measured the impact of our insights. The analytical team's bonuses were based on the impacts its insights had on the business, not the fact that it generated brilliant insights. This has been a major transformation for us. For instance, the analytical team used to set goals like: "Provide insights to the studios about how to improve user retention and make the games more social and fun." Now, our goals are: "Improve user retention by 10% this quarter." If retention only goes up 2%, no matter how good our insights, we don't achieve the goal.

One of our goals this past year was to help a game studio reach a certain number of daily mobile users. We planned several analyses that would help optimize different aspects of the game, and we did everything we said we were going to do. But in the end, the studio fell short of its target, so therefore we didn't hit our goal.

This can be frustrating. When I talked to my manager about our performance, I could easily have said, "Let's give ourselves a green because we did everything right." But I think that sends the wrong message. Instead, what I say is, "Though we did everything we said we were going to do, we clearly chose the wrong things to focus on." As a team, we discussed what went wrong and decided that we should have focused 90% of our effort driving cross promotions instead of everything else we did. In other words, we didn't choose the right driver of performance for the goal we wanted to achieve.

GETTING BUY IN FROM ANALYSTS

It takes a while for analysts to get used to the idea that we're holding them responsible for business outcomes. Since they only deliver insights and don't actually do the programming work, they often push back at first. They say, "We can't force the engineers to make changes. They don't report to us. And they often have different ideas and different priorities about what to do." I usually respond by saying that we need to be held accountable for outcomes, not insights.

To succeed, therefore, analysts need to become more skilled at influencing people. They need to be change agents, not just analysts. They must have strong communications skills. They can't just rest on their analytical skills. While analysts can strengthen their skills with formal training in statistics and quantitative methods, it's perhaps more important that they attend classes that teach communication and presentation skills. I know this sounds counterintuitive, but I truly believe it. Unless analysts can persuade business people to act on their insights, they don't contribute much value to the company. I prefer a trivial analysis done on a napkin that changes behavior to the most brilliant mathematical model that has no business impact.

SUMMARY

One of the biggest pitfalls of analytics is the one least discussed. That is, how easily we lose sight of the purpose of analytics. As Ken Rudin forcefully argues, the goal of analytics is not to create elegant statistical models or penetrating insights or even lots of action. The goal is to positively impact the business. Rudin shows how to shift an analytical culture from focusing on insights to delivering positive impact. The next chapter dives into the mechanics of creating analytical models, which can have the largest impact on the business of any technique in an analytical portfolio.

CHAPTER 13

HOW DO YOU DEVELOP ANALYTICAL MODELS?

Model-making is at the heart of analytics. Despite the mathematics that underlies statistical and machine learning models, analytical leaders say that creating effective analytical models requires a combination of art and science.

The art involves selecting variables that might correlate with a desired outcome. It also might involve allowing analysts to override statistical models based on their industry knowledge, as it does at Kelley Blue Book. Many companies today apply a combination of rules based on human experience (i.e., art) and statistical models (i.e., science) to optimize model outcomes. Our analytical leaders spend significant time discussing the role of art and science and other best practices for developing analytical models.

WHAT IS AN ANALYTICAL MODEL?

Few business people need to create analytical models or learn the statistical techniques upon which they're based. However, it is important that they know what an analytical model is and how it's created so they can better support the process or interpret the results.

An analytical model is simply a mathematical equation that describes relationships among variables in a historical data set. The equation either estimates or classifies data values. In essence, a model draws a "line" through a set of data points that can be used to group records or predict outcomes.

For example, a linear regression draws a straight line through data points on a scatterplot, showing the impact of advertising spending on sales for various ad campaigns. The model's formula—in this case, "Sales=17.813 + (.0897* advertising spend)"— enables executives to accurately estimate sales if they spend a specific amount on advertising. (See Figure 13-1.)

FIGURE 13-1. ESTIMATION MODEL (LINEAR REGRESSION)

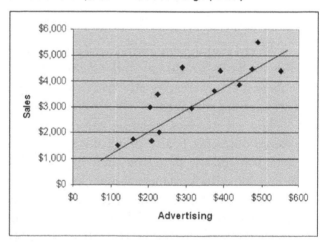

Advertising	Sales
$120	$1,503
$160	$1,755
$205	$2,971
$210	$1,682
$225	$3,497
$230	$1,998
$290	$4,528
$315	$2,937
$375	$3,622
$390	$4,402

An analytical model is a mathematical equation that draws a line through points plotted on a multi-dimensional graph.

Algorithms that create analytical models (or equations) come in all shapes and sizes. Classification algorithms, such as neural networks, decision trees, clustering, and logistic regression, use a variety of techniques to create equations that segregate data values into groups. Online retailers often use these algorithms to create target market segments or determine which products to recommend to buyers based on their past and current purchases. (See Figure 13-2.)

FIGURE 13-2. CLASSIFICATION ALGORITHMS

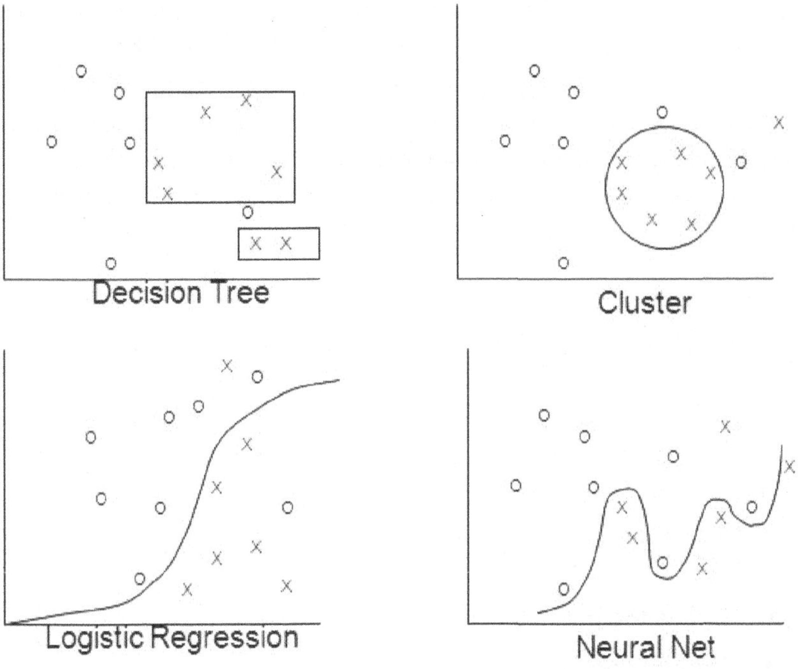

Classification models separate data values into logical groups. Each type of algorithm draws a different line through a set of data values.

Trusting Models. Unfortunately, some models are more opaque than others; that is, it's hard to understand the logic the model used to identify relevant patterns and relationships in the data. The problem with these "black box" models, such as neural networks, is that business people often have a hard time trusting them until they see tangible results, such as reduced costs or higher revenues. Getting business users to understand and trust the output of analytical models is perhaps the biggest challenge with advanced analytics.

To earn trust, analytical models have to validate a business person's intuitive understanding of how the business operates. In reality, many models don't uncover brand new insights; they simply surface relationships or patterns that people know exist but aren't top of mind. The models simply refocus people's attention on what's important. Of course, analytical models also uncover new, and sometimes startling, revelations.

For example, credit card companies used analytics to uncover a new source of fraud in which perpetrators use automatic number generators to guess credit card numbers at online sites. Their analytical models detected that a group of nearly identical credit card numbers generated an above normal number of transactions and lots of declines. Once the models surfaced this pattern, companies quickly identified the nature of the fraudulent activity and implemented the appropriate safeguards.

MODELING PROCESS

Given the complexity of advanced analytics, it's important that analytical modelers adhere to a methodology that is proven to generate accurate models. At a high level, the modeling process consists of six distinct tasks:

- Define the project
- Explore the data
- Prepare the data
- Create the model
- Deploy the model
- Manage the model

Interestingly, preparing the data is the most time-consuming part of the process, and if not done right, can torpedo the analytical model and project. "[Data preparation] can easily be the difference between success and failure, between usable insights and incomprehensible murk, between worthwhile predictions and useless guesses," writes Dorian Pyle in his book, *Data Preparation for Data Mining*.

In-database analytics. Traditionally, analysts download a data set to their desktop or local server to create analytical models. But this is changing. Many relational database management systems now embed many common data mining functions that enable analysts to do much of the exploration, preparation, model creation, and scoring inside the database instead of on desktops. This "in-database" approach speeds model development because analysts no longer have to move large volumes of data and manage cumbersome files. And it also improves model accuracy since developers can model all of the data instead of a sample.

1. Project Definition. Although defining an analytical project doesn't take as long as some of the other steps, it's the most critical task in the process. Modelers who don't know explicitly what they're trying to accomplish often don't create useful output. Thus, before they start, good analytical modelers spend a lot of time defining objectives, impact, and scope.

Project objectives consist of the assumptions or hypotheses that a model will evaluate. Often, it helps to brainstorm hypotheses and then prioritize them based on business requirements. *Project impact* defines the model output (e.g., a report, a chart, or scoring program), how the business will use that output (e.g., embedded in a daily sales report or operational application or used in strategic planning), and the projected return on investment. *Project scope* defines the "who, what, where, when, why, and how" of the project, including timelines and staff assignments.

For example, a project objective might be: "Reduce the amount of false positives when scanning credit card transactions for fraud." While the output might be: "A computer model capable of running on a server and measuring 7,000 transaction per minute, scoring each with probability and confidence, and routing transactions above a certain threshold to an operator for manual intervention."[2]

2. Data Exploration. Data exploration or data discovery involves sifting through various sources of data to find the data sets that best fit the project. During this phase, the analytical modeler documents each potential data set, if it hasn't already been done by a data analyst. For instance, they might identify:

---

2   From Pyle, Dorian, *Data or Data Mining*, San Francisco: Morgan Kaufman Publishers, Inc., 1999.

- **ACCESS METHODS:** Source systems, data interfaces, machine formats (e.g., ASCII or EBCDIC), access rights, and data availability.

- **DATA CHARACTERISTICS:** Field names, field lengths, content, format, granularity and statistics (e.g., counts, mean, mode, median, and min/max values)

- **BUSINESS RULES:** Referential integrity rules, defaults, other business rules

- **DATA POLLUTION:** Data entry errors, misused fields, bogus data

- **DATA COMPLETENESS:** Empty or missing values, sparsity

- **DATA CONSISTENCY:** Labels and definitions

Typically, an analytical modeler will compile all this information into a document and use it to help prioritize which data sets to use for which variables. A data warehouse with well documented metadata can greatly accelerate the data exploration phase because it maintains much of this information. However, analytical modelers often use external data and other data sets that don't exist in the data warehouse and thus must compile this information manually.

3. Data Preparation. Once analytical modelers document and select their data sets, they then must standardize and enrich the data. First, this means correcting any data errors that exist in the data and standardizing the machine format (e.g., ASCII vs. EBCDIC). Then, it involves merging and flattening the data into a single wide table, which may consist of hundreds of variables (i.e., columns). Finally, it means enriching the data with third party data, such as demographic, psychographic, or behavioral data that can enhance model accuracy.

Ideally, the data warehousing team creates an analytical data mart that generates data for the statisticians, saving them a bundle of time. However, as Dan Ingle discusses below, statisticians need to work closely with the data warehousing team and get involved in the data acquisition process. They need scope out new data and provide precise requirements about what they need, otherwise the data warehousing team won't be able to give them the right data in the right format.

From there, analytical modelers transform the data to meet the processing requirements of various machine learning algorithms. Common transformations include transforming categorical values into numerical values, normalizing numeric values so they range from 0 to 1, consolidating continuous data into a finite set of bins or categories, removing redundant variables, and filling in missing values. Modelers try to eliminate variables and values that aren't relevant, as well as impute empty fields with estimated or default values. In some cases, modelers may want to increase the bias or skew in a data set by duplicating outliers, giving them more weight in the model output. These are just some of the many data preparation techniques that analytical modelers use.

4. Analytical Modeling. Much of the craft of analytical modeling involves knowing which data sets and variables to select and how to format and transform the data to suit different analytical techniques and algorithms. Often, a modeler will start with 100+ variables and then, through data transformation and experimentation, winnow the number down to a dozen variables that are most predictive of the desired outcome.

In addition, an analytical modeler needs to select historical data that has enough of the "answers" built in with a minimal amount of noise. Noise consists of patterns and relationships that have no business value, such as the correlation between a person's birth date and age, which is a 100 percent match. An analytical modeler will eliminate one of those variables to reduce noise. In addition, they will validate their models by testing them against several samples from the original data set that they set aside in advance. If the scores remain compatible across training, testing, and validation data sets, then they know they have a fairly accurate model.

Finally, the modeler must choose the right analytical techniques and algorithms or combinations of techniques to apply to a given hypothesis. This is where the modelers' knowledge of business processes, project objectives, corporate data, and algorithms come into play. They may need to try many combinations of variables and techniques before they generate a model with sufficient predictive value. Every analytical technique and algorithm has its strengths and weaknesses, as summarized in Figure 13-3 below. The goal is to pick the right algorithm so you have to do as little data preparation and transformation as possible, according to Michael Berry and Gordon Linhoff in their book, *Data Mining Techniques: For Marketing, Sales, and Customer Support.*

FIGURE 13-3. ANALYTICAL TECHNIQUES

Technique	Use	Features
Linear Regression	Forecasting	Requires data that has no missing values or measurement errors.
Logistic Regression	Classification	Complex, but predicts the probability of an event occurring, so many business applications.
Clustering	Finds natural groupings in data; Often used to start an analysis	Unsupervised learning where the user determines the number of groups created; powerful and fast.
Decision Trees	Classification	Works with both categorical and numeric data; models are easy to explain.
Neural Networks	Prediction or classification	Complex and hard to use; values must be between 0 and 1 with no nulls; models are not easy to explain.
Ensemble Methods	Prediction or classification	Involves combining the output of many (possibly thousands) of models into a new output. The combination is often a better predictor than any individual model.

5. **Deploy the Model.** Model deployment takes many forms. Executives can simply review the model, absorb its insights, and use it to guide their strategic or operational planning. But models can also be operationalized. The most basic way to operationalize a model is to

embed it in a report. For example, a daily sales report for a telecommunications company might list customers for each sales representative by their propensity to churn. Or a model might be applied at the point of customer interaction, whether at a branch office or at an online checkout counter. (See Chapter 16 for more on deployment options.)

Scoring. To deploy models, you first have to score all the relevant records in your database. This involves converting the model into SQL or some other program that can run against the database that holds the records that you want to score. Scoring involves running the model against each record and generating a numeric value, usually between 0 and 1, which is then appended to the record as an additional column. A higher score generally means a higher propensity to portray the desired or predicted behavior. Scoring is usually a batch process that happens at night or on the weekend, depending on the volume of records that need to be scored. However, scoring can also take place in real-time, which is essentially what online retailers do when they make real-time recommendations based on purchases customers just made or pages they just viewed.

6. Model Management. Once the model is built and deployed, it must be maintained. Models become obsolete over time, as the market or environment in which they operate changes. This is particularly true for volatile environments, such as customer marketing or risk management. Also, complex models that deliver high business value usually require a team of people to create, modify, update, and certify them. In such an environment, it's critical to have a model repository that tracks versions, audits usage, and tracks compliance with internal and external regulations and policies. Once an organization has more than one operational model, it's imperative that it implement model management utilities, which most data mining vendors now offer. (See Chapter 16 for more on model management.)

COMMENTARY FROM ANALYTICAL LEADERS

 **THEARLING:** BUILD VS. BUY. When I was at Thinking Machines in the early 1990s, I firmly believed data mining would become a mass market technology. I was building data mining software at the time, and we believed such tools would eventually enable business users to push a button and get answers in a pop-up box. I remember feeling badly that we were going to put statisticians out of work! I truly felt that they were going the way of buggy whip makers.

But I don't believe this anymore. Although there is a lot of commercial data mining software today, you can never get rid of the statistician or at least the statistically-informed business analyst. You need these people to help identify the right questions to ask and the right data to analyze. Otherwise, you can easily produce garbage. Also, these folks need to monitor the models once they go into production to make sure the results are valid. Essentially, there's a lot of art involved in doing advanced analytics. You need artisans to create and maintain good analytical models. You can't mass produce them.

At the same time, there has been an explosion in analytics because it no longer requires a significant investment in time and money to do it. The data mining software I developed at Thinking Machines ran on a $25 million supercomputer! Today, it's much easier to create an analytically empowered organization. You can buy all the technology you need; you can purchase tons of data; you can hire consultants to do the work; and you no longer have to build everything from scratch. In fact, companies like Fair Isaac or SAS would be happy to provide you with a soup-to-nuts analytical solution.

REQUIREMENT FOR DOING BUSINESS. Basically, advanced analytics is quickly becoming a requirement for doing business, rather than a competitive advantage. If you have the will and the money, you can start an advanced analytics practice.

A few years ago, I attended a data mining vendor's customer advisory board meeting and heard a number of board members say that they were going to make significant jumps in their analytical sophistication in the next two years. A lot of their confidence came from the fact that the marketplace would provide them with the tools, people, and data they needed. I worked at

Capital One at the time, and it dawned on me that the competitive advantage we enjoyed from building an analytic capability from scratch at a sizable cost was now threatened. Any company could purchase an analytic capability. It was clear that advanced analytics was no longer a custom "build" market, it was a "buy" market.

SKILLED CRAFTSMAN. Nonetheless, as I said earlier, a statistician is a skilled craftsman. It takes years for a statistician to learn the trade— how to know which data set to use, which techniques and algorithms to select for particular problems, which variables to test, and what statistical pitfalls to avoid. And that's just the technical part of their job.

Statisticians also need to learn the business they're serving. They need to understand the nuances of the business processes they are trying to optimize and the underlying data. They need to learn which questions make business sense to pursue in the first place, and what model outputs make statistical sense but offer no business value. They need to learn how to communicate with business people to explain what the models have discovered and persuade them to adopt its results.

WORTH MILLIONS. So, although you can buy analytics, you can't buy this knowledge. A good statistician can be worth millions of dollars per year. That's the additional value they generate compared to out-of-the-box analytical models.

AVOID ERRORS

One thing that good statisticians do is to avoid injecting errors into analytical models that can have a big impact on the results. For example, I once saw an analyst accidentally flip the sign on the output of a model that identified the best customers to target with a new product offer. As a result, the model selected the worst customers instead of the best! This is a simple mistake to make, but it is easy to overlook if you are not paying attention.

Good statisticians also make sure that the data used to create a model is consistent with the data used when the model is in production, especially in environments where data is constantly changing. If an ETL job doesn't run properly or a production model points to the wrong variable in the database, you can get incorrect results. Or, perhaps the world changed since the model was created so the results no longer reflect the true state of the market. Good statisticians continually monitor the output of their models.

SIMPSON'S PARADOX. Good analysts are also careful about making inferences from the data. This is true even if you are looking at a simple summary, say in a crosstab report. For example, in Simpson's Paradox, you can see different results depending on how deep you look into your data. (If you don't know Simpson's Paradox, do a web search and read up on it. Anyone who works with data should understand this concept.) If you look at the top of a crosstab, you might get one result, but if you drill down one level, you might see the complete opposite result. If you are not paying attention, you can easily come to an incorrect conclusion that isn't fully supported by the data.

To avoid pitfalls like these, you might want to hold regular reviews where data analysts discuss mistakes they have made or seen due to misinterpreting data. Learn from your mistakes. The human brain is a huge pattern processor so you have to take steps to apply critical thinking to get the full value of analytics and avoid falling into hidden traps. We give people dashboards, crosstabs, and OLAP tools and tell them to make decisions using these tools, but we often don't teach them how to interpret the data or to avoid seeing patterns that don't exist.

TAYLOR: The key to creating effective models at Blue KC is to communicate continuously with the business units and track industry trends. This enables us to create models that solve business problems, rather than try to guess what the business needs.

We build and test a variety of analytical models in a sandbox within our analytical data mart. We then vet the most effective models with various business units to determine their ultimate value. We identify whether business units can use the model once, occasionally, or routinely. Models that can be used on a routine basis are operationalized in our analytical data mart. We maintain the one-time and occasional-use models in our sandbox and run them as needed.

BALANCING ART AND SCIENCE

 **INGLE:** We have a unique twist on the art and science discussion. We use science to acquire and prepare the data and generate statistical forecasts. On the art side, our analysts use their experience and judgment to interpret the forecasts when determining the vehicle values that we publish.

Our data management team ingests millions of records a week, largely from external sources, like auction houses and data aggregators. We feed this into SAS models that generate forecast coefficients in our vehicle information management system, which displays pricing curves. The analysts review the forecasts and can override the model output if they want; however they have to justify their decisions. So the heavy lifting is done by science and the nuance by industry expertise.

To review the forecasts, the valuation analysts use a homegrown slice/dice analytical tool to view and analyze the data fed into the models. They also talk to various people in the industry to get a sense of what's happening, including our field analysts, who attend large car auctions all across the country. They typically look for market anomalies that the statistical models may not have detected, such as an automobile lender that unloads a lot of Lexus ES350 automobiles that just came off lease, creating a supply imbalance that temporarily affects resale values in one or more regions. In essence, our vehicle values are quantitatively derived but qualitatively validated. We use a blend of art and science to generate the best analytical output for our consumers and industry customers.

Since moving to a more scientific approach for car valuations, we've also been able to increase the granularity and frequency of our forecasts. Seven years ago, we published monthly forecasts for three regions in the U.S. Today, we produce weekly forecasts for 51 U.S. regions, with more to come. And we've done all this without adding more valuation analysts. In addition, our models have low single digit error rates. But, like anything, there is room for improvement. This will be especially true when we forecast values for increasingly smaller geographic regions that don't generate a significant number of automobile transactions. So, our analysts and statisticians need to impute data when none or little exists and spend more time reviewing these values to ensure the best fit possible.

APPLYING AGILE TO STATISTICAL MODELING

One downside of embedding statisticians in the business units is that they have more demands on their time. So, we had to devise a way to ensure that statistical projects stay on track. After the data warehousing team introduced Scrum with great success, Shawn Hushman, who runs the enterprise analytics team, decided to apply Scrum to model generation.

Shawn taught his statisticians to develop models using three week sprints, small teams, and frequent interactions with business users. Of course, he put his own unique twist on the process, largely because statistical work is more project-oriented than data development work. For instance, our statisticians meet daily with each other instead of business stakeholders to get feedback on the models they're building; they use Gantt charts instead of storyboards to track timelines; they provide weekly, not daily, status updates to business stakeholders; and they present their findings in one-on-one sessions, rather than formal retrospectives.

These agile techniques help us better track the progress of statistical projects, so we know quickly if an embedded statistician needs help. Also, they give statisticians a step-by-step approach to development that helps break a big project into manageable pieces and avoid over-engineering a solution. Agile techniques also ensure that statisticians don't sit in their cubes all day without interacting with peers or business partners.

BEST-IN-CLASS STATISTICIANS. The best statisticians do analytical modeling from soup to nuts. They gather requirements, develop models, and deliver the results in a collaborative fashion. They understand that analytical models need to make business sense. So, they dig into the parameters to understand how each contributes to the whole and whether this raises any red flags. For instance, if a single variable contributes 50% to vehicle pricing, a good statistician investigates this anomaly and comes to business meetings ready to answer questions about it.

Although many statisticians have good technical skills, few have great business sense when they start out. To determine their business savvy, Shawn presents candidates for an open position in his department with three analytical models and asks them to pick the best one. Each model predicts the same thing and has similar error rates and variance. Most candidates drill into the minutia of the models, trying to find the one with the most statistical significance. But the real answer is, "The one that makes the most business sense."

Most candidates don't get the right answer, even those from the best universities. That's because most academic coursework simply doesn't teach students how to apply business sense to the statistical modeling process. To overcome this deficiency, Shawn seeds his statistical teams with experienced statisticians who can teach newcomers the business context required to create good analytical models.

 **COLSON:** Despite all the science involved in analytics, judgment and intuition still play important roles. Data scientists need to frame the business problem, choose the right modeling techniques—decision trees, clustering, regression, and so on—select the right data, define desired outputs and actions, and other salient factors.

When building models, good data scientists need to understand the variation in the data rather than merely account for it. They use intuition to come up with potential explanations for outliers and kinks in the data. Yet, they must be disciplined to frame their ideas as hypotheses that can be tested empirically.

For example, a data scientist trying to understand why a model didn't accurately predict a movie's success may observe anecdotally that the film's popularity appears to be driven by social media. He then hypothesizes that the number of Tweets the movie receives on Twitter is proportional to the movie's box-office revenue. A good data scientist typically has both the tenacity and the technical skills to acquire the data he needs to use in the model. Often, he fails to discover a statistically significant relationship which invalidates his hypothesis. But regardless of the outcome he learns. Each attempt at improving the model generates new knowledge about what works and doesn't. This knowledge accumulates and gradually gives way to better predictions.

EVOLVING MODELS. In the marketplace sometimes even tiny improvements to a predictive model can represent a material competitive advantage. It's an evolutionary process. Just as small changes in a species can give it a decided advantage as environmental conditions change over time, tiny improvements in model accuracy can help a company survive in a rapidly changing marketplace. Therefore, it is important to keep evolving and enhancing your models. As you do, it is imperative that you carefully measure the impact of each enhancement. Often, this is best done through A/B testing. Before rolling out an enhanced model, it's important to conduct an experiment that tests both the incumbent and enhanced models side-by-side using random samples. This is the only way to cleanly quantify the improvement due to the enhancement alone. This is important since there are typically other factors interacting at the same time, some of which can have a larger effect than the enhancement.

MODEL SELECTION. Accuracy is not the only characteristic to consider when selecting a model. Other characteristics include: transparency—or whether the model is easy to interpret; performance—the time it takes the model to run; and scalability—whether the model evolves as the business changes and grows. Every data scientist weighs these characteristics differently when selecting models. For example, I tend to prefer a transparent model slightly more than an accurate model that is harder to understand. These choices are subjective and can change over time, but good modelers make them consciously.

O'CONNOR: We use both deductive and inductive approaches when building models. The deductive approach starts with business questions and dives into the data to get the answers. For example, we may want to understand how consumers engage with an application over time and understand what causes their usage to grow or decline. Or we may want to track Web site traffic and predict traffic patterns in the future. Using this approach, our data scientists create models that are continuously updated with new data.

In contrast, the inductive approach starts with the data, which we explore to find interesting patterns and relationships. This type of modeling helps us answer questions that we have not even asked yet. This type of modeling gets us out of our comfort zone and usually inspires new ideas and ways of thinking about the business.

In either approach, it is critical to assess the quality of the underlying data, since our models are only as good as the data that populate them. Our team processes, labels, and catalogs data and builds connections between data sets to deliver a full picture of our consumers. Individual data scientists get involved in this process, as well, since they need detailed knowledge of the data upon which they are building models to ensure accurate outputs.

SUMMARY

Creating analytical models requires as much art as science. To get the best results, companies often apply a combination of statistical models and rules based on human experience and intuition. Much of the heavy lifting involved in creating analytical models involves exploring and preparing the data. A well designed data warehouse or data mart can accelerate the modeling process by collecting and documenting a large portion of the data that modelers require and transforming that data into wide, flat tables conducive to the modeling process.

The next part of this book (Part III) delves into the data and technical infrastructure that drive analytical solutions.

PART III
THE HARD STUFF: MANAGING DATA, ARCHITECTURE, AND TOOLS

CHAPTER 14

HOW DO YOU DELIVER QUALITY DATA FOR ANALYTICS?

It's been said, "The guy with the best data wins." Since data is the fuel for analytics, it's no wonder that analytical leaders spend a great deal of time gathering, organizing, documenting, and preparing data before they create a single pivot table, scatterplot, or linear regression. Without good data, there's nothing to analyze. Good analytical organizations are like professional house painters who spend 85% of their time scraping, sanding, and cleaning surfaces before they apply a drop of paint. Like good painters, analytical leaders know that without adequate preparation, all is for naught.

For most analytical leaders, data management revolves around data warehousing. Darren Taylor discusses how Blue KC replaced a marginally successful data warehouse to obtain an integrated view of corporate data, which executives recognized was critical to the company's strategy and growth. Dan Ingle explains how Kelley Blue Book's data acquisition team generates high-quality data for the data warehouse from 200+ external data feeds. Ken Rudin and Amy O'Connor emphasize the importance of instrumenting source systems to minimize data transformation work when populating data warehouses and other analytical systems.

Hard-core data scientists like Kurt Thearling recognize the importance of digging into the data. Thearling argues that data curation is the most important, yet underestimated, element of advanced analytics. Despite his 20 years of building analytical models, he'd rather talk about managing data than the newest machine learning algorithm. He knows that the adage "garbage in, garbage out" applies to analytics.

Exploring data with Hadoop. There are some instances, however, when it doesn't pay to spend too much time cleaning, modeling, and integrating data. This is when you just want to explore the data to see if it has any value to begin with. This is what makes Hadoop a valuable addition to the enterprise analytical ecosystem. Organizations can dump data into Hadoop that they couldn't afford to keep otherwise because it would have taken too much time to model and load the data into the data warehouse. With Hadoop, analysts who know how to write MapReduce code can explore the data, figure out what's worth saving, and get rid of the rest. They can then harvest the good data and load it into the data warehouse where users can analyze it with familiar SQL-based tools. This is a new and valuable workflow for turning raw data into an information asset.

Humpty Dumpty. Once an organization determines what data it needs, it faces another challenge: it has to collect and integrate data that runs on different systems in different formats both inside and outside the company. This can be a major task, similar to putting Humpty Dumpty back together again. It takes a lot of time to find the right pieces and glue them together properly. And like Humpty Dumpty, who perpetually climbs back on the wall only to take another nosedive, organizations also keep splitting their data into millions of pieces. Mergers and acquisitions, new executives and strategies, new technologies, and new regulations and competitors all conspire to fragment organizational data, making it a Herculean task to keep Humpty Dumpty whole and vital.

Data Flood. Moreover, the job of managing data is getting harder. Companies today are beset by a flood of data and new data types. Business users want more detailed transaction and interaction data to understand customer behavior and optimize operational processes. They want to fathom customer sentiment using email and text messages, as well as social networking data from Twitter, Facebook, LinkedIn, and other social media sites. They want to detect anomalies, threats, and opportunities using machine-generated data, such as sensors, geographical positioning systems, and radio-frequency identification tags. They want to track industry and market trends using third party transaction data. And they want to monitor dozens of new data-driven applications in the cloud, on the Web, and on mobile devices. In turn, organizations want all this data faster, so they can act more quickly to avert problems and exploit opportunities.

SYMPTOMS OF POOR DATA MANAGEMENT

Given this data deluge, managing corporate data is a full-employment opportunity. Not surprisingly, many companies struggle to build a solid data foundation upon which to conduct analytics. If your organization exhibits any of the following characteristics, it needs to spend more time on the basics of data management than implementing advanced analytics.

☑ Executives don't know how many customers the company has or how many it lost yesterday.

☑ Your company tries to retain customers who cost more money to support than they generate in revenue.

☑ Meetings degenerate into arguments about whose spreadsheet is right.

☑ New and old reports don't reconcile.

☑ Operational systems don't check the validity of data inputs across all fields.

☑ There is no single source that contains a comprehensive view of customers.

☑ Business people don't trust the data in standardized reports and dashboards.

☑ There are insufficient controls to ensure that employees can't see confidential data.

☑ The IT department owns and manages data definitions, not the business.

☑ Business users can't track the lineage of a report or dashboard objects.

☑ Analysts spend half their time gathering, massaging, and formatting data.

☑ Departments maintain their own data, even though they share data with other departments.

☑ There is no process for archiving or disposing of data that's no longer needed.

☑ There are thousands of reports with contradictory rules and definitions.

☑ No one was ever fired for misusing corporate data or violating established data policies.

Enterprise Data Strategy. Every organization, including those that treat data as a corporate asset, can cite a litany of data problems like those above. The difference between organizations crippled by data problems and those that harness data for competitive gain is awareness and policy. The latter acknowledge they have a data problem and have created an enterprise data strategy that defines the policies, procedures, and technologies to keep the data deluge from overflowing its banks, while the former drown in data problems, wasting valuable time, money, and resources delivering information to business users during each and every project.

The goal of an enterprise data strategy is to deliver the right data to the right people at the right time. In this sense, an enterprise data strategy is a far-reaching program that requires coordinated input from a variety of people and groups who administer or use data. An enterprise data strategy addresses the following areas:

- **DATA GOVERNANCE.** Establishes processes and procedures for creating, revising, and negotiating the definitions of shared data elements and metrics. Data governance is a business-driven endeavor in which business people (i.e., data stewards) assume responsibility for ensuring the semantics, integrity, and quality of key data elements.

- **DATA WAREHOUSING ARCHITECTURE.** Consists of conceptual, logical, and physical data models that represent how a business operates and programs that map data from any source to any target. Data architects also document the properties of data elements (i.e., metadata), including how data changes as it moved from source to target.

- **DATA ANALYSIS AND ADMINISTRATION.** Involves acquiring, documenting, and organizing data so business users can quickly find the data they need. Data administrators in the IT department ensure that data is properly formatted, stored, cleansed, and secured according to business policies established by data analysts in the business. In turn, data administrators work closely with database administrators who set up, manage, and tune databases.

- **DATA QUALITY MANAGEMENT.** Establishes business-driven programs to improve the quality of key data elements. Specifically, data quality programs create rules for validating and cleaning data that data administrators implement using data profiling, cleansing, and acquisition tools. Data administrators also monitor data acquisition jobs, manage errors and exceptions, and publish data quality metrics, among other things.

- **MASTER DATA MANAGEMENT.** Automates the process of standardizing reference data, such as customer, product, supplier, partner, and organizational hierarchies. MDM systems synchronize and match reference data captured by multiple operational systems, eliminating duplicate data and ensuring that every application uses the same data.

- **METADATA MANAGEMENT.** Defines the properties of shared data elements, including business and technical attributes as well as upstream and downstream dependencies. Armed with detailed metadata, data administrators can accurately assess the impact of any proposed data change, and business users can check the definitions of report objects.

- **SECURITY, PRIVACY. AND COMPLIANCE.** Companies place controls on sensitive corporate data to prevent unauthorized access, theft, or loss. They also mask confidential customer data to ensure privacy and archive data that they are required to retain and dispose of data they no longer need.

There is a lot involved in creating an enterprise data strategy. Although business people may sometimes question what they are paying for, a close examination shows that putting Humpty Dumpty back together again takes an inordinate amount of work.

COMMENTARY FROM ANALYTICAL LEADERS

O'CONNOR: We take an inside-out approach to data quality, which means we ingest any data we can get our hands on, irrespective of quality, and then whip it into shape. Our central analytics team partitions the ingested data to simplify access, and then works with the data owner to crack open the dataset. Next, our central team profiles the data to determine whether the records conform to an expected schema, if the volume follows an expected growth curve, and whether there are latency issues, which is particularly important given the global distribution of our data centers. These statistics give us insights into the quality of the data even before analysts consume it.

DATA QUALITY. The most important facet of data quality is its business impact. So we work with the business users to find out what fields they need and what measures of quality are important to them. We also work with data creators to raise the quality of the data generated by our source systems. Sometimes it's hard to work with Web log files because developers construct these files to debug their applications, not to help analysts gain insight about user behavior and activity.

For example, we tried to build a marketing application for our NavTeq map-based advertisers that showed the activity of our mobile phone users around their establishments. We bought some external advertising data and combined it with log data from our phones and maps. We dumped everything into Hadoop, ran MapReduce jobs to integrate and aggregate the data, and then visualized it. But the data wasn't in great shape and we didn't accomplish what we wanted. It was difficult to know how users were using the mapping application, because the Web logs were hard to understand and didn't map to application logic. So, we are trying to encourage developers to rewrite their logs so they we can use them to more easily track user actions and behaviors.

DATA DEFINITIONS. As a global company, Nokia also has to sort out cultural differences about the meaning of key entities. For example, we have to decide how to record an event that occurs at the same point in time around the world. For example, if the event occurs at 10 A.M. in China, but is time stamped by a server in the United States, what is the true "time" of the event? Data scientists need to take these issues into consideration when building their models.

THEARLING: People often want to jump into advanced analytics without doing the heavy lifting needed to analyze data efficiently and effectively. The biggest oversight they make is not curating the data. Data curation is about deciding what data to make available for analysis and organizing that data so that it's easy for users to find and access. It's more fundamental than data hygiene, which is about fixing data defects and errors.

DATA LIBRARIANS. I liken data curators to one of my favorite groups of people, librarians. I admire librarians because they make information accessible. They make decisions about what books to put in the library, where to put them on the stacks, and how people can find them. When you need a recommendation for a book, you can look to the librarian. Data curators, like librarians, are undervalued. Most companies don't invest in the big picture, and it eventually can come back to bite them.

For instance, without librarians, all the books in a library would probably be scattered on the floor. There would be no shelves, no Dewey Decimal system, and no one to help you find what you need. If by chance you find a pertinent book, you'd make photocopies of it and send them to your friends. The same is true with data. If analysts use whatever data is lying around, it eventually creates a mess that slows everything down.

For example, at Capital One, we built mission-critical analytical systems that scored customer records daily to support credit decisions. To operationalize that process, we made some hard decisions about what data to make available for the analysis. Before then, analysts could basically grab any data element they wanted. We counted tens of thousands of data elements in the system, which is comical, since we don't know that many things about our customers! So there was a lot of duplicate data and data of dubious value. Since a good model might only have 10 or 20 variables, analysts were spending way too much time combing through data elements to find ones that would make good predictors.

Subsequently, we asked our "data curators" to sift through all the data elements; they identified a much smaller number of relevant ones. We then gave analysts access to these variables from their data mining workbench. On the one hand, we took away some of their raw material, but on the other hand, we made sure that what we did provide was well managed, of high quality, and easily accessible. By curating the data, we lifted a big weight from their shoulders and made their jobs easier. They could focus on what they enjoyed doing rather than dealing with problems in the data.

When you let data get out of control, you have to invest more to get it back into reasonable shape. And it's an ongoing effort, because there are always new data sources to tap. For instance, a vendor once wanted to sell us an employability score that showed the likelihood that a person would have a job a year from now. That can be a useful piece of information if you're granting revolving credit, like we were. But the big question is whether that data was worth the money. The vendor wanted to charge something like a nickel a score. Someone on our staff had to figure that out whether that was a fair price. It's the same calculus a librarian uses when deciding whether to purchase a new book for a library.

MAKING DATA ACCESSIBLE. Once you bring in the data, you have to decide how to expose it to data analysts and statisticians. In other words, what columns do you show? You have all the data in the database, but what's worth showing the analysts? And how do you expose it?

For example, at Anvil Corporation, we built a data platform for doctors to analyze healthcare data sets. But healthcare data is messy and we wanted to hide its complexity. So we translated diagnostic and drug codes into plain

English and categorized them. Then, we discovered that drug codes from the Federal Drug Administration weren't very accurate, so we purchased better data from a third party. We did all this work just to populate a lookup table. But it was worth it. Once we finished, our physicians and biostatisticians were able to search for all antibiotics, instead of searching one drug at a time by its code. We also linked drugs with diagnoses to encourage doctors to think about the diagnostic capabilities of the drugs.

DATA CURATORS. So, data curation is about making sure you have the right data, that it's organized in a meaningful way, and that it's exposed in an optimal manner for users to access and analyze the data. Sometimes, the data curator's role is an extension of a data architect's. But most data architects focus on this critical task because it's tangential to do what they do. To be honest, it's hard to get resources to hire somebody to do this. You can probably hire a full-time person at a large company like Capital One, but at smaller companies, you usually need to make data curation part of someone else's job. In fact, it was part of my job at AnVil and I ran the department!

If I were to hire a data curator today, I'd look for someone on the business side who is a data analyst or statistician and likes to manage the process of moving data into their world. I'd shy away from data architects or administrators who sit on the IT side of things and control how data flows out of their world. You need to find someone who has seen the pain that happens when you neglect to curate your data. There are those who gravitate towards studying library science and serving as a librarian at a public library. You need to find someone with that same mindset, but who was originally a statistician. I should reiterate that a data curator does more than just attend to data quality issues. They have a much broader responsibility. They need to make business decisions about what data to maintain in your environment.

INGLE: We have relatively rigorous data governance and data management processes around our key data assets. Our data acquisition team creates reusable frameworks for ingesting data from external data sources, explores the condition and content of data, and establishes contracts for acquiring new data. Our data management team handles operational processes around our external data feeds, which tend to break with relative frequency. Our data providers inevitably forget to publish a file at the proper time, or forget to inform us about a format change, so we have to continually check what they haven't delivered and verify the layout. Since we run our models frequently, missing data in a feed can potentially alter the outcomes. To do this, we profile all the data feeds and measure their quality and condition. We automate many of these validations so that we get alerts when something exceeds a predefined threshold.

DATA CATALOG. Our data management team also manages our data catalog, which is our bible for data assets. It describes our data inputs, primarily from several external sources, as well as our data outputs. The catalog, which we maintain in Sharepoint, describes where each data set comes from, where it goes, how often we receive it, what it contains, who owns it, and whether there are any usage restrictions. For some of our larger, more critical data sets, we keep running counts of the number of records we receive from each source over a period of time.

STATISTICIANS AND DATA ACQUISITION. We work closely with our statisticians to ensure that we deliver the right data to them in a timely fashion. In fact, we feel it's important to give statisticians open access to data through its entire lifecycle. For instance, statisticians can access flat files in our staging area to determine whether the data is even worth moving into the data warehouse. Getting early access to raw data helps the statisticians better understand all the quirks of the data and provide clear instructions about how to dimensionalize it so they can use it. We also set up a host of sandboxes for statisticians inside the data warehouse where they can build production models.

Kelley Blue Book wouldn't be where it is today without a strong relationship between our data acquisition and statistical teams. This is not the case in most companies, where data teams zealously guard their data and keep statisticians at arm's length. When statisticians can't influence the shape of the data, they usually don't trust it, or they find that it's in a format that's unsuitable for modeling. Fortunately, our data and statistical teams excel at collaboration, which makes our modeling process very efficient and produces data that everyone trusts.

TAYLOR: From 2000 to 2003, Blue KC's IT resources were consumed with the Health Information Portability and Accountability Act (HIPAA). Our COO, CIO, and I got together and came to a quick consensus that our company needed to get its arms around its data. We believed that data was one of our company's most valuable assets, right behind people.

We had a data warehouse, but it wasn't hitting the mark—the data wasn't complete, integrated, or current—so people didn't use it much. This prevented us from insourcing critical programs, like medical management, which was part of our strategic direction. So, we decided to restart our enterprise data warehouse strategy, even though our existing data warehouse was only three years old. All together, we spent $2.5 million on consulting and about $4 million in total for the new program in year one. We didn't change our ETL tool, database platform, business intelligence (BI) tools, or our people; we simply changed our approach by applying tighter accountability and a shared business objective.

INTEGRATED DATA. The goal was to create an integrated source of information, updated daily, that would support all our operational and analytical requirements. To do that, we spent considerable time modeling our data along subject areas, such as claims, members, and providers. But we only tackled one subject area at a time to manage our scope.

For example, to build our claims subject area, we pulled in claims data from all parts of our business—pharmacy, dental, life, and medical. We harmonized the data and put it into a single fact table surrounded by several dimension tables that provided descriptive data about members and providers and other things. For the first time, our users could query all our claims data in one place and perform cross-functional analyses in a single query tool. This was a huge win. Next, we modeled and integrated our member and provider data the same way. Today, all our data is integrated and users can use one tool to access any information they need.

ANALYTICAL SNAFUS. Ironically, although we spent a lot of time and money building an enterprise warehouse for all our healthcare data, we never centralized analytics. Over the years, many of our departments had subscribed to various healthcare analytical services, and we ended up with several different analytical packages, each with overlapping functionality and models. Although we had a single version of truth in our data warehouse, we had multiple versions of analytical truth. Different departments would ask the same question and get different answers, even though all the data came from the same place. As a result, we ended up spending more time reconciling the numbers than acting on them. This was a big problem.

So, starting in 2009, our top executives began asking, "What's wrong here?

Why do we have this great data environment, but we can't excel in basic or advanced analytics?" It took us more than a year to agree on a course of action because department heads were afraid they might lose their business analysts if we centralized analytics.

We finally created a new division in mid-2010, called Enterprise Analytics and Data Management, which took charge of all the packaged analytic solutions, among other things. In short order, beginning in 2011, we deployed a new set of standardized analytical methodologies and built an analytical data mart to run the analytical models using data from our data warehouse. We implemented a Teradata appliance to power the analytical mart and installed MicroStrategy to deliver reporting, dashboarding, analysis, and visualization functionality.

As I mentioned earlier, we now resell this platform to other health plans who want to benefit from data warehousing and analytics. Some health plans are where Blue KC was before we implemented our data warehouse in 2004, and many are where we were before we created our analytical division in 2010. There's a lot of demand for analytical services, and we hope to cash in on that demand as well as deliver the best analytic solution possible for Blue KC.

RUDIN: We pay a lot of attention to data quality. But unlike most companies, we instrument data quality in our source systems. We don't have an ETL tool. Rather we push data directly from our games to our enterprise data warehouse in real-time. So, before we launch a new game, we build analytical tracking features into the game for all the things we want to analyze. We then build test suites to make sure that the games push out the correct data, and test it before the game is launched.

DATA DEFINITIONS. We also spend a lot of time discussing how to define data. For instance, it's not easy to define an origination point for a player when we calculate our daily summary metrics. The player could enter the game multiple times a day, each time from a different place, such as Facebook, a bookmark, or a URL string. This has big implications for how Zynga calculates various attributes associated with its key daily active user metric. After much discussion, we decided to use the player's initial origination point as their primary origination point that day. Although we track all origination points, we only use the initial origination point to calculate other metrics.

CREATING METRICS

We also learned that metrics should be simple so they can be easily understood by others. For instance, we created a metric that tracked system performance for Zynga's games. There are a lot of variables that contribute to performance, such as frame rates and the time it takes objects to load on the screen. We combined a half-dozen variables into a single metric, assigning a different weighting to each variable, and gave it a fancy name, like Total Performance Index, or TPI for short. The problem is that no one intuitively understood what TPI values indicated. They knew that lower numbers meant better performance, but couldn't grasp the significance of moving from a TPI value of 68 to 37. The metric was too abstract.

So, we divided this composite metric into its individual components and displayed those. We now have metrics such as "load time in seconds" and "number of frames per second." People understand these metrics. For example, they know that a 35 second load time is slow and a 7 second load time is reasonably fast. Since these metrics are easy to understand, people can more easily figure out ways to improve the performance of these metrics.

But we didn't stop there. We correlated metrics with our key goals and set thresholds for performance based on those goals. For example, to determine the correlation between screen refresh rates and Zynga's key goal of player retention, we conducted A/B tests. As a result, we identified the minimum acceptable refresh rate for each game, and we set our metric thresholds accordingly. The key is to make metrics simple and actionable. With a good metric, people intuitively know what it means, how it correlates with goals, and what actions to take to move it in the right direction. Defining good metrics is critical to delivering good quality data.

SUMMARY

The ultimate goal of an enterprise data strategy is to create sustainable processes that bake data quality and consistency into the culture of the organization and deliver a standard set of enterprise data across business functions. This only happens when the business views data as a corporate asset and develops an enterprise data strategy, working with the data team to implement it.

Traditionally, the centerpiece of the enterprise data strategy is a data warehouse with consistent data definitions and conformed dimensions. Yet, many companies struggle to build and evolve data warehouses quickly and cost effectively. The next chapter unveils the secrets of creating an agile data warehouse that adapts quickly to changing business conditions.

CHAPTER 15

HOW DO YOU CREATE AN AGILE DATA WAREHOUSE?

One of the knocks against data warehouses, which are critical components of any analytical ecosystem, is that they are slow to build and change. This is understandable once you recognize that the purpose of a data warehouse is to deliver a unified view of enterprise data and serve as the foundation for all reports and dashboards used to make decisions. This sounds easy, but is hard to do.

Virtual view. Data warehouses deliver a "single version of the truth" for an organization. With a well-designed data warehouse, there is no dispute about what different metrics and data elements mean. And users have one place to go to get a comprehensive and integrated view of business activity, even if the data is generated by a multiplicity of internal and external systems that use different file formats, data definitions, and aggregations. A good data warehouse cleans up a multitude of organizational and computational sins and places a shiny data veneer on top of a fragmented mess. It is a virtual representation of the state of the business.

Adaptable systems. But organizations are constantly in flux. There are mergers and acquisitions, reorganizations and restructurings, new strategies and directions, and new products and services. Change is constant. And that means the data warehouse has to change with it. But how do you build a system that always changes? How do you maintain a single version of truth when the truth is evanescent? This is the challenge of the data warehouse, and that's why they take so long to build, maintain, and evolve.

Given this context, analytical leaders have devised many innovative ways to make data warehouses more agile. For example, Ken Rudin shows how to capture rapidly changing game features without altering a data warehousing schema. His secret is to embed key-value tables inside the data warehouse to handle volatile data. Eric Colson takes the opposite approach and uses a concept he calls "eventual cohesion" to rapidly evolve the data warehousing schema and keep up with fast-changing business requirements. Other analytical leaders use data vault modeling, Scrum development, and a myriad of other techniques to accelerate data warehousing development.

Harmonization. However, none of these techniques change the fundamental, top-down nature of a data warehouse; nor should they. Organizations need to complement top-down data warehouses with bottom-up analytics to support the diverse information needs of an organization. As we'll see in Chapter 17, an analytical ecosystem harmonizes the conflict between control and creativity and centralized and distributed development in data-driven environments. Despite what skeptics say, the data warehouse is here to stay. If you need proof, listen to the analytical leaders in this book describe the role of the data warehouse in their analytical environments.

DATA WAREHOUSING DEVELOPMENT

In general, data warehouses have an image problem. That's because a data warehousing environment is like an iceberg. The business only sees a small fraction of the work involved in creating one. Consequently, business people often don't appreciate the work that goes into building these solutions—or to borrow an analogy from the previous chapter—"put Humpty Dumpty back together again."

The data warehousing framework in Figure 15.1 depicts the

percentage of time required to build each layer in a data warehousing solution. The application layer—which is the only layer that business users see—consumes only 10% of the total time required to build a data-driven solution. In contrast, logical modeling consumes about 30% of the time, and the physical data integration consumes the remaining 60%. These percentages vary based on the condition of the source data that needs integrating and the degree of consensus among business users about the definitions of key metrics, dimensions, attributes, and hierarchies.

FIGURE 15.1. DATA WAREHOUSING FRAMEWORK

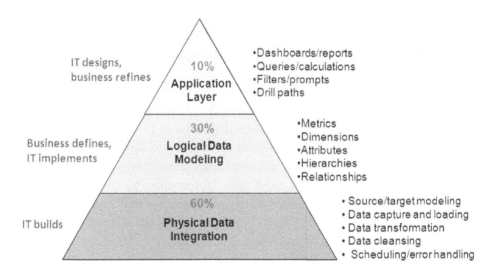

The quickest part of a data warehouse to build is the application layer that business users see; the most challenging part is the logical layer that requires functional leaders to come to consensus on data definitions; and the most time-consuming part to build is the physical integration layer.

Politics. Although logical modeling consumes roughly 30% of project time, politics often makes it the hardest to accomplish. Getting the heads of sales, finance, and marketing to agree on the definition of "customer", "sale", or "lost customer" can be torturous, and only a CEO can usually resolve the standoff. However, getting consensus for a departmental solution is easy, since departmental users typically see the business in the same way and use the same lexicon and rules to define business activity. That's why companies enjoy greater success building departmental solutions than enterprise ones.

The other difficulty with logical models is that they are not easy to change. That's because changes to these models often break downstream applications that rely on them. Thus, it's imperative for data warehousing managers to maintain accurate information about data model dependencies. Also, some models become extremely complex so that changing or adding attributes or relationships in the model triggers a cascading series of changes. However, as Rudin and Colson show below, there are ways to gracefully accommodate change without slowing down the business.

Accelerating development. Once an organization models and loads a majority of its core data in the data warehouse, it reaches a tipping point in which the time and cost of delivering data warehousing-driven applications plummets. Here, business users recognize that the data warehouse is the only database that delivers a truly integrated view of the organization, and they start using it to develop enterprise applications and conduct cross-functional analyses. In addition, a fully loaded data warehouse enables data developers to build new applications more quickly since all or most of the data they need is already integrated, formatted, and sanitized. Unfortunately, most of these benefits don't accrue until after an organization has made a significant investment of time and money to populate their data warehouses with data spanning all subject areas in the business.

Nonetheless, analytical leaders have devised many ways to keep the data warehouse current while continuing to add new subject areas and data to meet evolving business requirements.

COMMENTARY FROM ANALYTICAL LEADERS

KEY VALUE TABLES

 **RUDIN:** One dilemma Zynga faced early on was how to create an agile data warehouse. Zynga adds new features to its games daily and weekly, so it couldn't modify its data warehousing schema fast enough to keep up. To address this problem, we came up with a unique approach: we applied all changes in a key-value store so we didn't have to change our data warehousing schema.

Today, Zynga has an HP Vertica data warehouse that stores two kinds of data. The first is non-volatile data whose attributes don't change, such as player IDs, player profiles, and certain game attributes. This is about half of its data. It dumps everything else into a key-value table in a Vertica relational database. This wide, flat table has a bunch of columns with generic data types. For example, it might have 20 number fields, 10 string fields, and five date fields. Developers can use the fields any way they want. But typically only they know the structure of the data that they dumped into the key-value table, and only they know how to interpret the data they get back from a query. Because there is no structure to this data, Zynga can't run standard reports against it, but individual developers can query it.

For example, say Zynga introduces a bartering feature into a game that lets two players exchange goods, but doesn't have a way to store these barter transactions in its data warehouse schema. So, a developer loads these transactions into the key-value table in the data warehouse. The developer uses the first number field for the transaction ID, the second number field for the number of items exchanged, the first text string field to describe the bartered items, and the date field to define the date of the exchange, and so on.

The powerful thing about a key-value table is that another developer can use these same fields in an entirely different way. As long as developers create unique keys to identify their records—and we have a convention for doing this—they can query their data and grab just the records they want. If developers frequently implement the same attribute or set of attributes in the key-value table, we'll eventually add them to our standard data warehousing schema so developers don't have to create custom definitions of those attributes for each analysis they do.

Zynga's standard reports run only against the non-volatile data stored in standard relational tables. But users who want to analyze new game features filter the relevant records from the key value pair table. This means they need to know the keys of records they're looking for and how that data is structured so they can write relevant SQL to extract and manipulate the data. Obviously, this requires some SQL skill and knowledge of the data and its content. But this a clever way to store lots of data quickly in a SQL environment that changes very quickly.

EVENTUAL COHESION

COLSON: A huge challenge in enterprise-scale data warehousing is accommodating change. Parts of the data model are constantly evolving through usage and iteration. At the same time, data teams continually add and modify new data sources. I use the term "eventually cohesive" to describe how to balance agility and integration.

Ideally, all subject areas in a data warehouse connect to each other, share common keys and dimensions, and never get out of sync. But this describes a monolith, and monoliths move slowly. So, if you hold out for a 100% cohesive data model, you pay a big price. It's a Pyrrhic victory. By the time you complete or update the data model, business people have moved on because their requirements have changed and you neglected all the other things they wanted to do. In other words, you achieve data cohesion but at too great a cost. Your rigidity and unwillingness to accommodate change forfeited business value.

You need to let go of the goal of constant cohesion, and instead embrace the notion of "eventual cohesion". This philosophy accepts ephemeral states in the data model where things are not 100% aligned. You accept this in order to move more quickly and deliver more value. Yet, it doesn't abandon the notion of an integrated data model. At any point in time, there are parts of the data model that are in flux, but they always evolve towards cohesion – not divergence.

For example, we often added new subject areas to the data warehouse to support departmental initiatives. We never exactly knew how to organize new dimensions upfront but that didn't stop us from changing the model. We simply watched how the business used the data, and once those usage patterns became clear, we finalized the dimensions and connected the tables into the enterprise model. The key is that we wouldn't spend a week or month to conduct an exhaustive requirements study. We delivered value immediately and discovered the true requirements as we went along, even if that meant creating non-conforming dimensions for a while. This is what I mean when I say "eventually cohesive."

SOCIAL COHESION

Eventual cohesion can happen naturally when developers embedded in business departments share the same enterprise data model. In this environment, developers must collaborate with each other because they all use the same core entities. None of them wants to be responsible for adversely affecting the work of another so they become good at communicating changes they need to make. They also know that they will benefit when someone adds a new attribute or fact to a core entity that they all share. Thus, data developers have a vested interest in working together to coalesce their subject area data models.

Also, by establishing standards and best practices, designs can naturally align even when developed without collaboration. For example, data developers can easily and willfully follow naming conventions, data types, and design patterns. They don't mind adhering to these standards because it saves them time. The developers say, "Just tell me the naming convention and the data types so I can get going." These "contextless" standards don't impair their ability to apply creative solutions based on their rich business context.

CHANGE MANAGEMENT MEETINGS. To ensure that this social cohesion occurs, it's important to provide a forum in which data developers from every department present the changes they need to make to the enterprise data model. Collectively, they discuss how to make the changes to minimize costs and disruption for all. The developers don't ask permission to make a change; rather they inform others what needs to be done. For example, a team may say, "We're changing these 20 tables, here's why, and this is what you need to do." The onus is on the initiating team to identify the impact of the change on everyone else. In some cases, the initiating team may even make the changes on behalf of the impacted teams to speed the process.

EASIER TO FIX THAN TO PREVENT. The eventually cohesive approach comes with some risk. The occasional snafu may occur. For example, a team might launch a new data structure that hasn't been properly tuned and as a result slows down queries. But this can usually be remedied quickly and often has only minor consequences. If you try to prevent all problems, you can slow progress, impair the business, and frustrate your most talented developers who have low tolerance for rigid processes.

The moral of the story is that it is often easier to fix a problem than to prevent it. Sometimes, data professionals get too caught up trying to achieve perfection when they are better served making a few mistakes. You learn as you go along and that's invaluable. Processes designed to eliminate mistakes stifle discovery and innovation. You can't always move in unison because that is too slow. The eventually cohesive approach lets data developers charge ahead on a new project without having to wait for the entire data warehouse to move with them.

SUMMARY

Innovative analytical leaders have devised numerous ways to adapt data warehouses to rapidly changing business conditions. Unfortunately, business users only see a small fraction of the work that goes into building a data warehouse and don't always appreciate what's available. But, organizations that invest in data warehouses for the long haul reap the benefits of having an integrated view of business activity.

Another critical piece of the data infrastructure is the processes and systems required to deploy analytical models developed by statisticians and data scientists. This is the focus of the next chapter.

CHAPTER 16

HOW DO YOU DEPLOY ANALYTICAL MODELS?

We learned in Chapter 12 that the value of analytics is not the insights it delivers, but the impact it has on the business. In this chapter, we discuss how to implement analytical models so that the business benefits from them.

Kurt Thearling, a long-time data scientist, argues that the real challenge is not creating analytical models, but deploying them. While serving as Vice President of Strategic Technology at Capital One, Thearling learned the importance of managing models throughout their lifecycle, from creation to deployment to retirement. He recommends that companies with multiple production models establish a governance strategy that deploys models in an efficient fashion and ensures that they comply with all privacy, security, and other regulations.

Model governance requires companies to implement a repository for storing, managing, and documenting models that enables administrators to control user access, audit usage, manage versions, and release certified models into production, among other things. If done right, model governance can give companies a competitive advantage in the marketplace. This chapter is devoted to Kurt's comments on model governance and deployment strategies.

DEPLOYMENT OPTIONS

But before turning to Kurt's perspective, which comprises the entire commentary below, it's important to understand the various ways that organizations can implement models and act on their results. The options range from sharing the results in a meeting to embedding models in applications and automating decisions.

Present the model. The first way companies can implement an analytical model is to present the results to executives in a meeting. By exposing unobserved patterns and trends in the data, models can help executives see the business in a new light and help them shape new go-to-market strategies. For example, a police chief might assume that drugs are the primary driver of criminal activity in his city, but a model that shows that most crime centers around racetracks and gambling parlors. This insight might cause the chief to shift resources from catching drug dealers to investigating mob-related activities.

Embed in reports. Another approach with broader distribution is to embed models in regularly scheduled reports. For example, one retailer embeds the results of a churn model into a weekly sales report distributed to front-line salespeople and their managers. The report graphically displays which customers are likely to churn in the near future in a manner that is intuitive for salespeople to understand. In this case, the report designers applied "smiley" and "sad" faces to customer records based on their scores across several variables in the model, including the classic retail marketing indicators of recency, frequency, and monetary. (See Figure 16-1.)

According to the director of analytics at the company, "We had to make the model digestible for the sales people since they speak in terms of average order size, not R-squared values."

FIGURE 16-1. A WEEKLY SALES REPORT WITH EMBEDDED CHURN MODEL

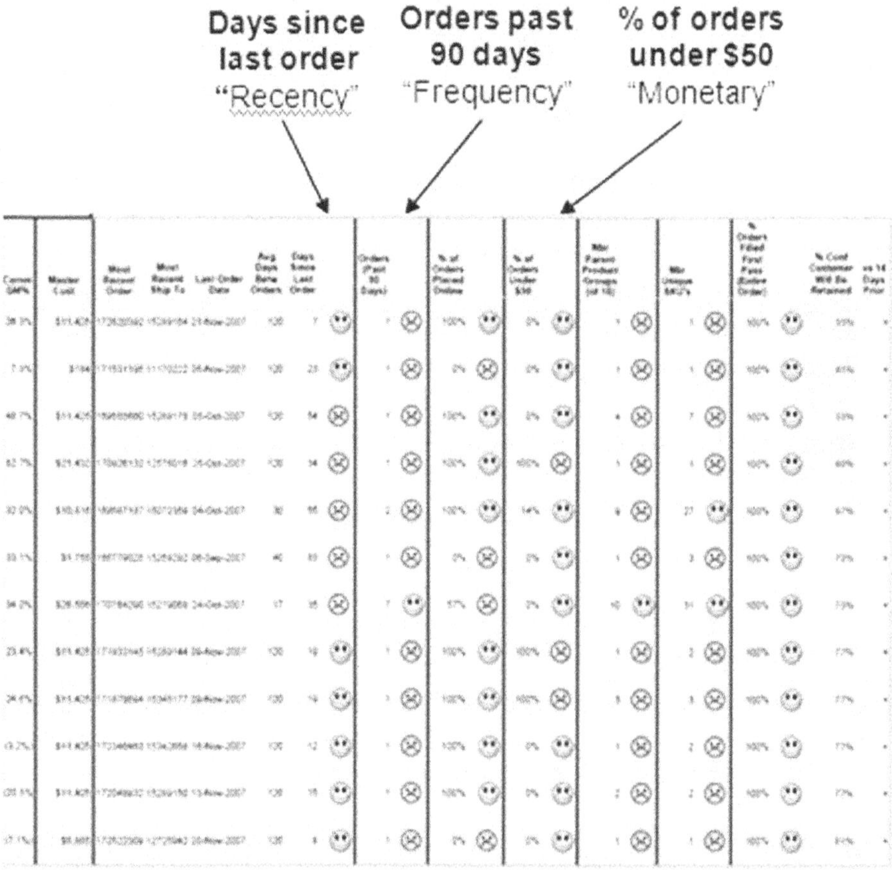

Embedding the output of analytical models into sales reports requires some creativity to express the insights in terms that salespeople can understand and which make sense from a business perspective.

Embed the model. Another way to deploy a predictive model is to embed it into an operational application so that new events (e.g., a customer transaction) automatically generate recommendations (e.g., cross-sell offers). In some cases, an application feeds these recommendations as a script to a customer service agent who delivers the offers verbally to a customer. In other cases, the application delivers the recommendations to the customer without human intervention.

The triggered actions (e.g., recommendations) can be based on a model score, which is generated in batch or real time. In a batch environment, a company runs the model each night against all customers in its database and assigns each record a score between 0 and 1. In a real-time environment, the score is generated automatically based on the customer's historical transactions, Web pages they recently viewed, or items currently in their shopping cart.

At the point of interaction, the application either looks up the batch-generated customer score or creates the score in real-time. The application then inserts the score into a rule, and then executes the rule to determine the action. For instance, a Web recommendation engine might create the rule, "If a customer who purchased product "X" exhibits a product affinity score of 0.8 or higher, then display pictures of the following items with the text, 'You may also be interested in purchasing these other items.'" Some rules are based entirely on model scores, while other rules use scores as one element among many variables, such as the time of day, type of customer, or type of product.

Decision Automation. When applications trigger actions without human intervention, this is called "lights out" decision making or "decision automation." In some respects, decision automation is the holy grail of analytics, although it's not generally applicable. Decision automation works when applied to stable processes with a proscribed set of outcomes. For example, a model might automatically approve a customer's request for a credit limit extension. Or, a model might detect fraudulent transactions and recommend actions based on the characteristics of the transaction.

In reality, however, many decision automation applications involve some form of human intervention, including the examples cited above. For instance, a fraud model will kick out suspicious transactions for a human to investigate, or a credit model will send applications with a variety of exigencies to an underwriter to evaluate. On the other hand, Web recommendation engines generally don't involve human intervention, although marketing analysts generally monitor the effectiveness of their recommendations several times a day and make changes to the models if conversion rates drift downward.

COMMENTARY FROM ANALYTICAL LEADERS

PUTTING ANALYTICAL MODELS INTO PRODUCTION

THEARLING: In some ways, the easy part of analytics is developing models. The hard part is deploying them, especially in a large-scale operation that generates tens of millions of scores a day. It takes most companies weeks or months to deploy models. If it takes a long time to implement a model, the model could be out of date before it even goes into production What you need is a production analytical system that automates the deployment of models.

At Capital One, we built industrial systems that automatically scored models from our model repository, recovered from failures, and fed the output to various downstream systems, all with minimal human intervention. These systems gave us a huge competitive advantage that was worth tens of millions of dollars.

Some of these systems generated millions of scores a day in big, batch jobs and spit out the results to various downstream systems. Others were online systems that generated automated credit decisions while customers were on the phone with a call center agent. These so-called "decisioning systems" could grab customer account data, run it through a scoring model, and display a recommendation to the agent in less than a second.

MONITORING MODELS. Of course, once you put a model into production, someone still has to watch it to make sure it continues working as intended. This is where the modeler as craftsman plays a role. For example, various things in the marketplace can affect the accuracy of a model. In fact, all models go bad over time because the world changes. A modeler needs to decide when there has been enough change to warrant rebuilding the model. Also, mistakes can happen that affect model outcomes. For example, a data feed can break or a transformation rule can get corrupted. Only a skilled statistician or analyst can detect such problems early in the process and make changes before problems arise. The bottom line is that an analyst's job isn't done once they write and test a model; he has to monitor and manage the model through its entire lifecycle.

THE IMPORTANCE OF MODEL GOVERNANCE

MODEL REPOSITORY. Once a model has been built, it is important to govern and keep track of that model as you move from development to deployment. This is where a model repository comes in. The repository tracks equations, variables, and data fed into a model and makes it easy to do impact analysis. So if you lose a source of data, you can query the repository and discover all the models that use that source. This is a much better alternative to collecting the models in a paper binder and putting it on a shelf. If the building burns down or the analyst leaves the company and there is no one who can decipher what they wrote, the company is at risk.

CLASSIFYING MODELS. Model governance ensures that you don't put models into production without the necessary checks and reviews. First, you evaluate the models and classify them based on their business impact. For example, a class four model might have a critical impact on the business, and therefore require the chief statistician and his deputy to review and approve the model before it is put into production. A class one model, on the other hand, might have a much smaller impact and only require sign off by a peer. Once you understand the business importance of a model, you can then apply appropriate resources to decide if and when to move it into production.

METADATA. Model governance also involves tools and procedures for managing versions of models, controlling who can access, edit, and deploy models, and auditing changes. Today, these features are built into the model management modules of most commercial data mining software, from vendors such as SAS or SPSS. Sometimes, you'll hear statisticians complain that these tools don't offer as much power as writing statistical code from scratch, and that's probably true. But they are self-documenting, which can be critical. They keep track of who created, edited, approved, and ran the model, which equations and data were used, and so on. This information is useful if something goes wrong and you need to investigate.

For example, a former colleague once told me about a problem at his previous employer. The bank he worked for bought a data feed that provided bankruptcy scores, and they used that data to make credit decisions. Later, due to corporate cost cutting, the company stopped buying the data feed. Someone checked with the analytical teams that used the data, and each said it was fine to discontinue the data feed. However, there was one model that they missed. When the company eliminated the data feed, the column went blank, and the production system no longer identified people with risky financial histories. As a result, the bank loaned tens of millions of dollars to people who should never have qualified for a loan.

You can argue that someone should have known about the model's dependency on this data feed, but people are human and make mistakes. More commonly, people leave companies and their knowledge of how the systems work disappears with them. To avoid human error, you need automated systems that track this information.

If you are just doing exploratory data analysis and haven't put models into production on a large scale, then you probably don't need to be overly concerned about model governance. But once you start using models to make significant business decisions that drive revenue, you need to do this. It is just the smart thing to do.

Fortunately, it's a lot easier to manage models today than ten years ago when most of the tools just spit out an ASCII file and you could do whatever you wanted with it. At Capital One, I pushed our vendors to implement model governance features and we sponsored proof-of-concept projects to move this idea forward. Many data mining tools now offer these features.

TURNING REGULATIONS INTO A COMPETITIVE ADVANTAGE

In some industries, legal, regulatory, and governance policies have a tremendous impact on analytics. This is true for banking, insurance, healthcare, pharmaceuticals, and others. It is a fascinating area; one that I didn't see before I arrived at Capital One.

At Capital One, I built a lab to evaluate new analytic tools and techniques and figure out how we could deploy them in a highly regulated business. This wasn't simply a matter of building or buying a new algorithm. It was figuring out how the algorithm works, and how to integrate it with our statistical environment. It also meant working with lawyers and risk managers to make sure the model's results would comply with federal regulations. This was a non-trivial problem, and one that we became quite good at solving.

MODEL GOVERNANCE. One of the first things you need to do is keep track of your analytics. If you are a bank, the Office of the Comptroller of the Currency (OCC) requires you to maintain records of every model you've ever produced and who approved them. You may need to accredit your scoring officers so they are authorized to approve models before they go into production. When you start generating statistical models, you have to be careful.

The fascinating thing about model governance is that it can give you a competitive advantage. It's easy for companies to get bogged down in regulations regarding the proper use of data. If you know how to navigate the legal and regulatory issues surrounding analytics better than your competitors, you can roll out models faster, using more sophisticated techniques.

In a large organization, you often get data from different places, and you have to be careful about how you collect and share data across internal boundaries. In a financial services company, you may have a variety of relationships with an individual customer. You have bank accounts, an auto loan, and a mortgage. If you want to use analytics to figure what other products to offer the individual, you have to make sure you aren't violating any legal rules in your use of the data.

So you end up playing the game of twenty questions with the lawyers. They'll ask, "Did you collect the information for a student loan?" "Was the amount over $5,000?" "Is the parent a loan borrower?" Depending on your answer to those questions, you might not be able to use the data to cross promote other products. As corporations grow, the decision tree of questions grows with them.

AUTOMATING COMPLIANCE. It's a non-trivial effort to keep track of all the regulations and laws that constrain how you can use data in an organization. At Capital One, we built a system to manage this. The analyst could provide the answers to a series of questions about how data was collected, hit a button, and learn whether they were allowed to use the data or not. By automating this process, we shielded the modelers from having to deal with these sorts of things, which is not what we hired them to do.

Related to this is how you deconstruct models to satisfy regulatory requirements. For instance, when a bank makes a credit decision, it needs to generate a Principle Reason for Adverse Action (PRAA), which is sometimes called a "turn down reason." If you turn someone down for credit, they have the right to ask why you turned them down. By law, you have to give the person a simple answer, and regulations require that the answer contains just a single variable.

For example, you cannot say, "Given your bankruptcy, you have too many open lines of credit." That answer has two correlated variables. You either have to say, "You have had a bankruptcy" or "You have too many open lines of credit." It is not easy to deconstruct all models in this way, and it complicates the process. Knowing how to do this for the kinds of models in use at your business is critical. If you're good at this, you can use more complex models than your competitors to make business decisions because they don't understand how to navigate the relevant regulatory issues.

SUMMARY

Analytical models don't deliver value until they are put into production. There are many ways to deploy models, from presenting the results in a PowerPoint presentation to embedding them in reports or applications. Companies can even use models to automate decision making in stable processes. However, there is a lot of work involved in deploying analytical models, especially in companies that produce many of them. To get the most out of the models, companies need to establish a model governance strategy that manages and deploys analytical models in an efficient, secure, and compliant fashion.

The next chapter rounds out the infrastructure required to implement analytics. It provides a reference architecture for an analytical ecosystem that merges top down and bottom-up approaches to analytics.

CHAPTER 17

HOW DO YOU ARCHITECT AN ANALYTICAL ECOSYSTEM?

For more than two decades, analytical professionals have tried to shoehorn diverse types of business users, workloads, and data into the same analytical architecture, often with disappointing results. The problem is that analytics is a broad domain. Strategically, it's about using information to make smarter decisions; tactically, it's about building reporting and analysis applications.

Analytics consists of two fundamentally different approaches to generating insights. A top-down approach generates reporting applications for casual users, while a bottom-up approach supports ad hoc inquiries by power users. These two approaches support different users, workloads, design frameworks, and architectures; yet, they are interrelated. Analysis leads to reports, and reports trigger new questions that require analysis. Companies that harmonize top down and bottom up approaches to generating insights succeed with analytics. (See Figure 17-1.)

FIGURE 17-1. TOP-DOWN VERSUS BOTTOM-UP ANALYTICS

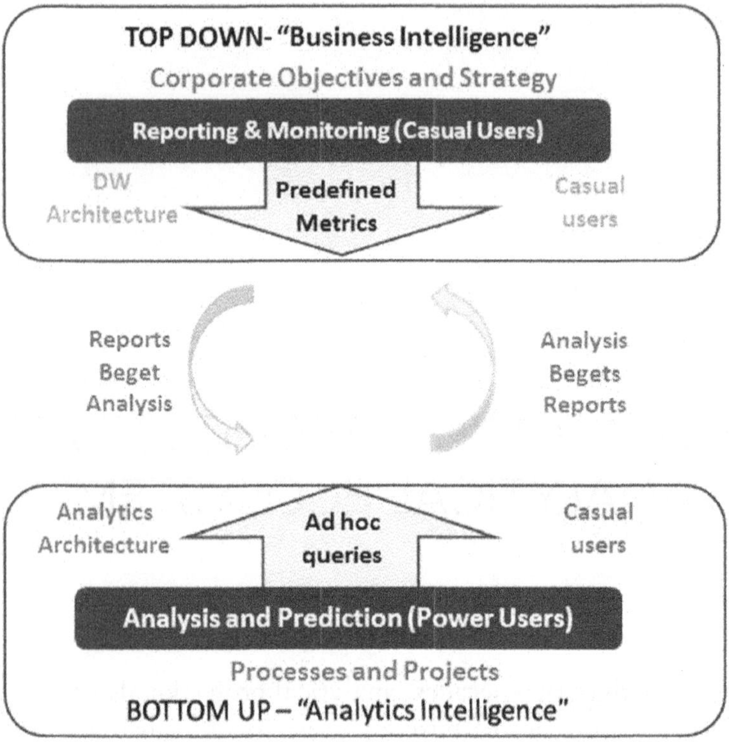

Top-down and bottom-up analytics create a synergist environment. Organizations must create an analytical ecosystem that supports both approaches to analytics in a coherent, integrated fashion.

Top down. Another term for top-down environment is "business intelligence." Here, business users monitor business activity using strategic and tactical metrics embedded in reports and dashboards. The target users of these reports and dashboards are "casual users"—business people who consume information to do their jobs, such as executives, managers, and front-line staff. To design reports and dashboards, developers discover which questions casual users want to ask, and then they find the appropriate data, model and transform it, and load it into the data warehouse.

Top-down environments standardize the definition of data elements shared across business functions. Developers use this data to create a virtual representation of the business and then bake the model into the data warehouse. Thus, a top-down environment takes a lot of time and money to build and requires consensus among business unit heads about the meaning of shared business metrics, dimensions, attributes, and organizational hierarchies. (See Chapters 14 and 15.) As a result, top-down environments take a significant amount of time, money, and political capital to build and, thus, are hard to change. However, they ensure a consistent mapping of enterprise information, which is a key requirement among executives who want to run their businesses using a single set of numbers.

Bottom up. In contrast, analysis is a "bottom-up" environment in which business analysts, statisticians, and data scientists use a variety of tools to explore data, test hypotheses, and answer unanticipated questions from business executives. Traditionally, these analysts or "power users" gather, integrate, and manage their own data, define metrics and data elements independently, and distribute their findings as reports or dashboards to the rest of the organization.

Unlike the top-down world, a bottom-up environment is quick and inexpensive to build and deploy. It's also easy to change because it typically consists of an individual analyst with a spreadsheet or inexpensive analytical tool who doesn't coordinate his work with anybody else. In the same way, entire departments often create their own reporting and analysis applications independently of other departments or corporate reporting initiatives. Unfortunately, this activity creates lots of analytical silos, or "spreadmarts," that eventually flood the organization with duplicate and contradictory data. These silos eventually overwhelm analysts with unwanted data management tasks and suffer scalability and performance issues.

Challenges. One of the primary challenges with analytics is that organizations—whether consciously or not—tend to flip-flop between top-down and bottom-up approaches. When data warehouse-driven reports and dashboards become too slow and costly to deliver, or fail to provide rich, ad hoc exploration or modeling capabilities, organizations turn to bottom-up analysis tools. When the bottom-up tools "hit the wall" because they can't scale and deliver consistent data, they revert to top-down tools. Organizations that chase their analytical "tail" never reap the full benefits of analytics.

Data developers in the top-down world tend to view analysts as the "enemy" who sabotage their efforts to deliver a single version of the truth to the organization. In contrast, analysts in the bottom-up world often resent data developers and IT administrators who block access to corporate information resources. As a result, analysts spend many hours crafting ways to circumvent IT policies and procedures so that they get the data they need when they need it. Rather than viewing each other as analytical cohorts, these two groups distrust, and, in some cases, despise each other.

THE NEW ANALYTICAL ECOSYSTEM

To resolve this tension and reconcile top-down and bottom-up approaches to analytics, organizations need to recognize that they need both to succeed. They need to harmonize top-down and bottom-up analytics within a single environment that delivers the best of both worlds while minimizing their downsides.

Figure 17-2 depicts a reference architecture for a new analytical ecosystem. The objects in dark gray represent the traditional business intelligence and data warehousing environment, while those in light gray represent new architectural elements made possible by new big data and analytical technologies.

FIGURE 17-2. THE NEW ANALYTICAL ECOSYSTEM

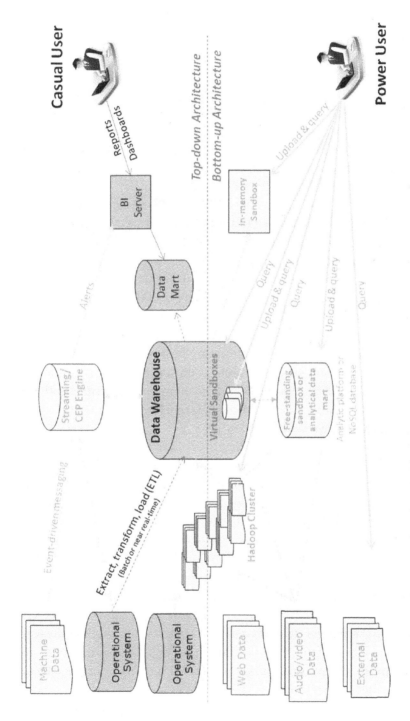

The new analytical ecosystem combines top-down and bottom-up approaches to analytics into a seamless whole, while making power users full-fledged members of the environment through various types of analytical sandboxes.

By extending the traditional business intelligence (BI) architecture, organizations gain the best of top-down reporting and bottom-up analysis in a single ecosystem. Traditionally, reports and analyses run in separate environments—reports using data warehouses and analyses using Excel, Microsoft Access, and desktop visualization tools. But the new analytical ecosystem brings these two worlds together and gives both casual users and power users (i.e., analysts) suitable means for accessing enterprise information and analytical resources.

Hadoop. In this new conjoined environment, much of the source data flows through Hadoop, which acts as a staging area and online archive for an organization's data. This is especially true for multi-structured data, such as log files and machine-generated data, but also for some voluminous types of structured data, such as call detail records, point-of-sale transactions, and insurance claims, that companies can't afford to store and process in their atomic form using SQL databases. From Hadoop, much of the data is fed into a data warehousing hub, which then distributes data to downstream systems, such as data marts, operational data stores, analytical appliances, and in-memory desktop databases, each of which enables users to query data using familiar SQL-based reporting and analysis tools.

Top-down Monitoring. The top-down world depicted in the top half of Figure 16-2 consists of the classic business intelligence architecture, along with a complex event processing (CEP) engine that monitors high-volume event streams, such as those emanating from sensor fields, stock market feeds, or point-of-sale terminals. CEP engines are rules-based notification engines that monitor an event stream and trigger alerts or kick off internal workflows when they detect a predefined pattern of events. For instance, many credit card companies use homegrown or commercial CEP engines to detect fraud, and government agencies use CEP to detect intrusions and fraudulent activity on their computing networks. The bottom line is that top-down environments enable casual users to monitor business activity using metrics aligned with business objectives.

Analytical sandboxes. The bottom-up world of analysis depicted in the lower half of Figure 17-2 makes power users full-fledged members of the analytical ecosystem. They are no longer treated as second class citizens who must beg or fill out forms in triplicate to access corporate information and analytical resources. The new analytical ecosystem gives them four analytical sandboxes in which they can query and explore corporate data without interfering with other analytical workloads:

- **HADOOP.** Stores large volumes of atomic-level unstructured and structured data that data scientists query using procedural or Hadoop-specific languages.

- **VIRTUAL DW SANDBOX.** A partition, or set of tables, inside a data warehouse, dedicated to individual analysts who can upload their own data and mingle it with corporate data.

- **FREE-STANDING SANDBOX.** A high-performance analytical system, either SQL-based or not, that contains either a replica or subset of data in the warehouse or completely unique data.

- **IN-MEMORY SANDBOX.** A desktop visualization tool that lets analysts download data from the warehouse, combine it with their own data, and publish the results to a corporate server, if permitted, for casual users to consume.

Different types of analysts use different sandboxes. Data scientists query raw, multi-structured data in Hadoop using Java, Python, Perl, Hive, or Pig. Business analysts query virtual sandboxes in the data warehouse or analytical data marts using SQL or SQL-based tools. Statisticians use data mining functions built into free-standing analytical platforms to create and run data mining jobs. Business analysts download data into an in-memory database on their desktop or a local server and use visualization tools to explore the data at the speed of thought.

Combining enterprise and local data. Virtual DW sandboxes let power users upload their own data to the data warehouse and mix it with corporate data. This provides the best of both worlds, since corporate data warehouses often don't contain all the data that analysts need to unearth answers to challenging questions. Also, by centralizing analyses, analytical sandboxes eliminate data shadow systems and give analysts greater visibility into each other's work, fostering collaboration and reuse which saves time and money. The only catch is that analysts must agree not to distribute the results of their findings as published reports, which creates new spreadmarts and adds to information chaos. Rather, they need to work with corporate data developers to transform their analyses into scheduled reports for others to consume.

The new analytical ecosystem reconciles the top-down world of reporting and the bottom-up world of ad hoc exploration into a seamless whole, while making power users full-fledged members of the enterprise analytical environment. Not every analytical leader has implemented every facet of this reference ecosystem, but several are heading in this direction.

COMMENTARY FROM ANALYTICAL LEADERS

O'CONNOR: To deliver analytics as a service, Nokia decided to store as much data as possible in one place and push the development of insights to the business units. Not surprisingly, big data and Hadoop are core to our architectural strategy. The economics of Hadoop make it possible to put petabytes of data in one place and process it efficiently. Most of that data is unstructured, including search and map logs.

However, our commitment to Hadoop doesn't mean we're throwing out our existing data management systems. Nokia is a large company with 60,000 employees, and we've built a lot of data warehouses and data marts over the years. We will continue to support these data structures because they contain most of our structured data and a lot of business logic. People also know how to query data in these systems using SQL-based tools. Hadoop enables us to offload some processing from these systems and avoid costly upgrades.

For instance, we have log data from our phones that we use to track the number of devices that have been activated in the last 30 days. That data is voluminous. So instead of trying to push all the data into our corporate data warehouse, we now flow it into Hadoop, where we parse and aggregate the data and push the summaries to the data warehouse for reporting and analysis. This has enabled us to cost effectively store raw event data, while continuing to exploit the business logic that has been built up over the years in the data warehouse.

ARCHIVE AND STAGING AREA. Currently, we view Hadoop as an archival and staging area as well as a gigantic sandbox for analytics and reporting. Generally, we filter, parse, and aggregate some content in Hadoop and push it into various data warehouses and data marts so people can analyze the data using familiar SQL-based tools. And our data scientists conduct analyses directly in Hadoop using Hive and Pig interfaces. We run Hbase to support some of our transactional mobile applications. Basically, we don't dictate the tools that business units use to analyze data. We simply collect and manipulate data in Hadoop and then feed the aggregates to whatever tools they want. We are ecumenical that way.

We are also building a catalog of our data assets in Hadoop to make it easy for people to find relevant data. The catalog describes attributes for each data set; how data sets are transformed, aggregated, or combined; and when those jobs ran and what data they touched. Analysts can browse the catalog to find relevant data for their analyses. Along the way, they might discover someone else has already done some relevant analytical work and they reuse those data sets, saving time. In essence, our data catalog is critical to turning our data into an asset that we can productize.

TAYLOR: The data warehouse at Blue KC has 12 years of atomic data, and we continue to add new subjects to increase the richness of the analysis and reporting we can do. For instance, in 2006, we began collecting more data about employee health. We began conducting biometric screenings of our customers' employees, as well as having them fill out an annual 60-question health assessment. We also now load clinical data into the data warehouse, including lab and other clinical data from doctors' offices.

By adding these new data types and subject areas, we've been able to better support medical management initiatives and patient-centered medical homes. We now work proactively with chronically ill patients to get them to a stable state faster, and coordinate with all their medical providers to ensure they stay healthy longer. Because the data warehouse integrates all our data, we can assess risk factors for each member, display them in a dashboard, and use the data to take action to improve health or avoid catastrophic and costly illnesses.

DW HUB. We use our data warehouse more for operational reporting than iterative analysis. The IBM DB2 data warehouse supports 34 subject areas that are populated daily with data from 70+ data sources. The data warehouse contains a lot more data than we need to run analytical queries and is not tuned to deliver fast, iterative responses. But it is good for running short tactical queries against operational data, as well as large batch jobs, such nightly ETL processes that feed downstream systems. So, the data warehouse is basically a hub that feeds clean, integrated, consistent data to specialized data marts, such as our analytical data mart and Web data mart, which have distinct data models and data structures.

ANALYTICS. Our new analytical mart, which consolidated analytical models and applications running in numerous business units, is geared to slicing, dicing, and drilling using MicroStrategy's reporting and analysis tool. Each month, we push a subset of the data from the data warehouse into the analytical data mart. The analytical data mart runs a variety of models on the new data and feeds the resulting scores to both the BI server (MicroStrategy) and back to the data warehouse, which preserves a history of predictive scores for every member.

So the data warehouse serves as the repository of historical data, while the analytical mart handles most of the reporting and analysis. The analytical mart runs on a high-performance analytical appliance from Teradata that gives users a fast, iterative analytical experience. In contrast, our Web mart runs on Microsoft SQL Server, which supports indexes for high-speed individual transactions. These aren't bite-sized marts; they are very big databases that support unique workloads.

RUDIN: Zynga meticulously measures user activity on our sites so we can better understand the way players engage with our games. As a result, Zynga captures tens of billions of rows of data every day, which we analyze to better understand the impact of our games.

BIG DATA VIA SQL. When we built our corporate data infrastructure two years ago, most people said that SQL databases couldn't handle large-scale data. They recommended that we use Hadoop because it is highly scalable, flexible, and well suited to Web log data— all of which were key requirements for us. However, in the end, we decided to buck conventional wisdom and go with a SQL database, specifically Hewlett Packard's Vertica, to fuel our analytics infrastructure.

A major reason we did this is because most of the queries we run are dimensional—for instance, we examine player actions by game by time sliced by number of friends, and so on. Each of those descriptive attributes is a dimension. Since SQL is optimized for running dimensional queries, we decided to stick with SQL as much as we could. Plus, everyone knows how to use SQL or graphical tools that generate SQL under the covers. Although Hadoop is more flexible and works on a broader set of problems, it's not optimized for running dimensional queries.

SQL AT SCALE. We figured out how to create a SQL-based architecture that avoids the scale and schema problems associated with relational databases. The reason Web log data is so voluminous is that it contains a lot of extra stuff you don't need. For example, we only wanted to capture information about user actions in our games, which are stored as parameters at the end of URL strings. So, rather than processing 50TB of daily Web log data to pull out the 5TB of data that we really want, we decided to bypass Web logs and transformation programs altogether. Instead, we programmed our operational systems (i.e., our games) to write data directly to our data warehouse. This amounts to about five terabytes a day, which most high-performance SQL databases can handle. So, when a player does something in one of the games, such as log in, visit a game neighbor, or message a friend, these events are captured and written to the data warehouse in near real time.

This approach eliminates the need to capture and process huge volumes of Web logs and then load the results into a data warehouse. These processes are complex, time-consuming, and costly. The downside of the approach is that you have to add tracking code to the gaming applications so that you can write data directly to our data warehouse.

DYNAMIC SCHEMA. Another problem we had to overcome is what I call the "static schema" problem. We typically issue one or two new releases of each game a week. Designers are constantly adding, deleting, and modifying game features. Ordinarily, we would have to modify our data warehouse schema to accommodate these changes, but given the rate of change within our games, it would have been impossible to keep up. So, we decided to store our non-volatile data in a fixed relational schema and our volatile data as key-value pairs in a massive table in Vertica. (See Ken's commentary in Chapter 15 for more detail.)

HIGH PERFORMANCE PROCESSING. Zynga relies almost entirely on open source software to power its game platform and analytics infrastructure. The two main exceptions are Vertica, which runs the data warehouse, and

Tableau, which analysts use for visual analysis and exploration. To get the proper performance, Zynga caches a lot of stuff in memory. It doesn't have an ETL tool. The team guarantees that it will clean, deduplicate, and load game data into our data warehouses within 10 minutes. Zynga also does real-time streaming of every major metric about its games and players, so we know almost immediately whether there is an abnormal dip in traffic, and this triggers alarms using our open source alerting software.

Zynga has two instances of our data warehouse, one for operational reporting, and the other for ad hoc analysis. The reporting data warehouse runs our production reports and dashboards, written using Tableau and home-grown tools. In contrast, the second data warehouse serves as a sandbox environment where analysts run ad hoc queries. In addition, Zynga gives general employees access to a sample data set that contains about 1% of all data in the data warehouse, and we give our trained analysts access to 100% of the data.

LEONARD: When I arrived at U.S. Xpress, the company ran largely off of spreadsheets. We had thousands of spreadsheets in the company. I know, because I did an inventory of them. We posted that inventory on a wall to show people where we've come from and where we're going. We've eliminated a lot of them, but still have a ways to go.

We decided to front-end the data warehouse with an operational data store (ODS). The ODS provides near real-time data, which is the lifeblood of a trucking company. For instance, our XPM system enables fleet managers to monitor hundreds of trucks in their region and optimize schedules, routes, and orders in real time. So the ODS helps these managers make quick decisions and adjust to reality on the road faster.

The ODS is merely a set of normalized set of tables running in the data warehouse that stores about 24 hours of data. We cleaned up the customer data in the ODS and now use it to feed the XPM fleet management system as well as our data warehouse, our CRM system, and various mobile dashboards. So, the ODS is the near real-time hub that delivers a consolidated view of customer data to any application that needs it. You can call it our master data management (MDM) hub, if you want. We recently expanded the content to include assets and locations.

MESSAGING. To support our operational applications, we built a service-oriented messaging architecture that pulls data from source systems using Microsoft BizTalk, including sensor data from our trucks that comes in via satellite, WiFi, or cellular connections and publishes it to other systems. We purchased data integration and data quality tools from Informatica, which has a BizTalk connector, to filter, clean, match, standardize, and integrate relevant data from the event stream and load the ODS. We also have many cubes and reports that give our executives and fleet managers easy access to the data they need. And many of these are available through Apple iPads. The tools promote self-service report creation, so users get the data they want when they want it.

NEAR REAL-TIME DASHBOARD. The first application we built was an executive dashboard that tracks the time our trucks stand idle every day. We pulled attributes generated by our DriverTech system, which is a ruggedized on board computer that captures everything from speed, location, and braking events to engine performance and cabin temperature, and transmits the data wirelessly to our data centers. By consolidating and displaying this telemetric information, we reduced truck idle rates and saved the company a lot of money in fuel costs.

Mobility is such a natural for us at U.S. Xpress so we built it into the fabric of our architecture; that's why we capture and deliver data in near real-time and display many of our reports and dashboards on mobile devices.

EDI. We are moving to frictionless orders. This is where an order comes in through electronic data interchange (EDI) and is automatically routed, based on rules, to the right planner to make a decision about whether to accept the order or not and how to combine it with other orders. We now combine orders in our XPM application with analytical information about customers, routes, and drivers to help managers make those decisions.

For example, a fleet manager receives a freight order originating in Atlanta. He checks our driver scorecard and sees that one of his best drivers is headed there. The manager can dispatch the order to that driver via an iPhone app or our onboard DriverTech system, instead of waiting for the driver to reach his destination and call in for a new assignment. This is a win-win for everybody. The driver gets a choice assignment and we get the best driver for the job.

Personally, I believe every organization needs to implement a near real-time, mobile architecture. But there is a lot of inertia out there. Even at U.S. Xpress, our Vice President of Engineering initially didn't think we needed real-time, mobile applications. But now he has a list of mobile applications that he wants me to build.

SUMMARY

Harmonizing top-down and bottom-up worlds is not easy, but it's a critical step in delivering a robust analytical ecosystem that fully serves the needs of both casual and power users. The new analytical ecosystem provides suitable infrastructure to support any kind of reporting and analysis application the business requires. Perhaps a tougher question than how to architect an analytical environment is what analytical tools to purchase. That's the subject of the next chapter.

CHAPTER 18

WHAT ANALYTICAL TOOLS SHOULD WE USE?

Interestingly, our analytical leaders weren't particularly interested in talking about tools. The only exceptions were Tim Leonard and Darren Taylor who touted the benefits of delivering dashboards to executives and managers via tablet computers. At both their companies, business users enthusiastically embraced mobile dashboards, giving the analytics team added credibility and momentum.

FITTING TOOLS TO USERS

When it comes to selecting tools, it pays to know your users and how they prefer to consume information. Most user populations divide into casual users and power users. Savvy analytical managers map these groups and their requirements to suitable analytical tools. (See Figure 18-1.)

FIGURE 18-1. FITTING USERS TO ANALYTICAL TOOLS

	80% of the time		20% of the time	
CASUAL USERS	Task	Tools	Task	Tools
Executives	Monitor	MAD Dashboard	Create queries	Superusers (Excel, BI search, voice-enabled BI)
Managers	Analyze		Create plans	
Front-line workers	Drill to detail		Create reports	
POWER USERS	Task	Tools	Task	Tools
Superusers	Ad hoc reports	Self-service BI	Monitor Analyze Drill to detail	MAD Dashboard
Business analysts	Explore, plan, visualize	Viz tools, Excel, SQL		
Statisticians	Create models	Data mining tools		
Data scientists	Explore Hadoop	Java, Perl, Hive, Pig		

The dark shading refers to bottom-up (i.e., ad hoc or exploratory) analytics, while the light shading refers to top-down analytics (i.e., monitoring and reporting). The tools and tasks listed for power users are generally additive as you move down the hierarchy.

Casual Users. Casual users, such as executives, managers, front-line workers, customers, and suppliers, use information to do their jobs. About 80% of the time, casual users want to monitor key metrics, so a performance dashboard is ideal for them. The best dashboards are layered information delivery systems that give users a quick graphical, summary of performance against key metrics, but enable them to drill to any information in three clicks or less. These MAD (monitor, analyze, drill to detail) dashboards are becoming pervasive in the top-down world of analytics.[3] (See Chapter 2.)

---

3 See Wayne Eckerson, *Performance Dashboards: Measuring, Monitoring, and Managing Your Business*, Second edition (Wiley, 2010) for more information about the MAD framework and tips and techniques for implementing dashboards.

The challenge with casual users is meeting their ad hoc requirements the other 20% of the time. To be honest, most casual users today don't have the patience or technical savvy to use self-service features embedded in reporting and analysis tools. As a result, they often turn to superusers to create ad hoc reports for them. Over time this will change, as a more tech-savvy generation of workers enter the workforce and as new technologies, such as BI search and voice-enabled queries, become mainstream.

Power users. Unlike casual users, power users get paid to crunch data on a daily basis. Information is their job. They include super-users, business analysts, analytical modelers, and data scientists. (See Chapter 8 for a description of these roles.)

As a whole, power users are skilled craftsmen who need specialized tools for every imaginable analytical job. Would you hire a carpenter to build an addition on your house if he arrived with just a hammer in his toolbox? Of course not! In the same way, analysts need a plethora of tools at their disposal. For instance, they need Excel for planning, SQL for ad hoc queries, mashboards for creating ad hoc reports and dashboards, OLAP for dimensional analysis, visual discovery tools for exploration, data mining tools for analytical modeling, and Java, Perl, Python, Hive, or Pig for manipulating Hadoop data.

Not every analyst needs every tool. Superusers are the predominant users of self-service BI tools and mashboards, while business analysts use Excel, SQL, and visual discovery tools. Statisticians use data mining tools, while data scientists use Hive, Pig, and various programming languages. As analysts expand the scope of their analyses, they often pick up new tools to meet their information requirements.

Figure 18-2 plots different categories of analytical tools for power users against data scalability and calculation complexity. Tools in the upper right quadrant offer the highest levels of data scalability and calculation complexity.

FIGURE 18-2. THE SPECTRUM OF ANALYTICAL TOOLS

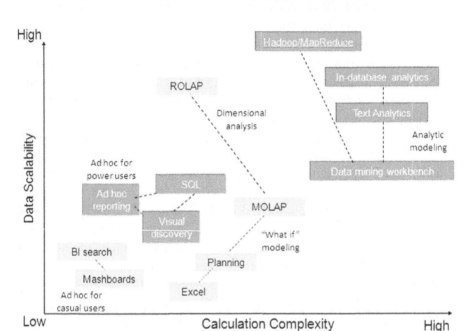

This chart plots various categories of analytical tools against the dimensions of data scalability and calculation complexity.

CONSUMERS VERSUS PRODUCERS

Another way to map users to tools is to examine the functionality required by information consumers and information producers. Consumers consume information, while producers produce it. Casual users are always consumers, rarely producers. Power users, such as analysts, statisticians, and data scientists, are both consumers and producers, usually in equal proportion. Data developers are primarily producers.

Analytical tools provide different levels of support for consumers and producers. Figure 18-3 shows a hierarchy of self-service functionality for information consumers and producers. As you move down the consumer hierarchy, tools deliver greater interactivity and analytical capability. As you move down the producer hierarchy, the tools provide more sophisticated design, development, and administrative capabilities. The best tools expose this functionality on demand to avoid overwhelming users with too much functionality all at once.

FIGURE 18-3. SELF-SERVICE HIERARCHIES

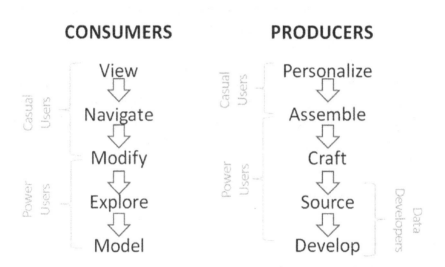

There are two types of self-service, one for information consumers and the other for information producers. Each consists of a hierarchy of functionality that gets exposed on demand. The Consumer hierarchy exposes greater levels of interactivity and analytical capability, while the Producer hierarchy exposes greater levels of development and administrative capabilities.

Consumer self-service. Generally, casual users stick to the top three levels of the consumer hierarchy. For example, an executive might *view* simple static dashboards on a tablet computer and click once in a while to *navigate* or switch dimensions. But a manager might also want to *modify* an existing table or chart by sorting or ranking the data or adding a calculated column, such as a subtotal for a group of records. Power users, on the other hand, will spend most of their time in the bottom three levels of the hierarchy where they can *modify* existing data sets or create custom groupings, *explore* data visually, and create statistical *models.*

Producer self-service. In the producer hierarchy, casual users may occasionally *personalize* the look and feel of a report or dashboard by changing colors, fonts, and chart types. Superusers often *assemble* dashboards by dragging predefined tables and charts from a library onto a dashboard canvas (i.e., mashboards) or *craft* an ad hoc report using the semantic layer of a reporting tool. Business analysts will also assemble and craft reports and dashboards, but they also may *source* new data using a query generator or by writing custom SQL and importing the data set. Data scientists may *develop* code to create a complex query or report, while data developers might write a script to create a custom application with unique functionality, workflow, and look and feel.

The benefit of mapping out self-service hierarchies is that you can map these to requirements when selecting analytical tools. It's best to find analytical tools that enable administrators to expose these different levels of functionality to users on demand, once they are ready and able to use them. Otherwise, the additional functionality can overwhelm them and cause them to stop using the tools.

SUMMARY

It's ironic that our industry focuses so much attention on tools and technology, when our analytical leaders emphasize the importance of people and processes to analytical success. Most analytical leaders believe it's possible to succeed with almost any technology available today. However, they also believe that good tools in the hands of the right people can make a big difference in user satisfaction and productivity. Whenever possible, analytical leaders try to stay ahead of the technology curve and equip users with the latest tools and technologies.

CHAPTER 19

WHAT'S THE ROLE OF BIG DATA IN YOUR ENVIRONMENT?

"Big data" is one of the most hyped technology trends in the past 20 years. Even though the core technology driving the big data phenomenon has barely emerged from the lab, early adopters are jumping on the bandwagon, and nearly everyone else is kicking the tires or scratching their heads trying to figure out what big data is and how to benefit from it.

Our analytical leaders are fairly representative of the larger community. Some have fully embraced Hadoop as an enterprise staging area (Netflix, Nokia); some have applied it tactically to augment parts of their data flow infrastructure (U.S. Xpress); some have investigated it but chose another strategy for handling big data (Zynga); while others have yet to evaluate its potential (Kelley Blue Book, Blue KC). And Eric Colson describes Hadoop as a mini-rebellion by application developers who find SQL and data warehousing approaches too restrictive, inflexible, and slow.

THE ROLE OF HADOOP

In the broader marketplace, big data has become synonymous with Hadoop—an open source framework for parallel computing that runs on a distributed file system (i.e., the Hadoop Distributed File System or HDFS.) For the first time, Hadoop enables organizations to cost-effectively store and analyze *all* their data, including semi-structured data, such as Web server logs, sensor data, email and extensible markup language (XML) data, as well as unstructured data, including audio, video, images, and text. In contrast, relational databases are best suited to handle just structured data.

Some say Hadoop is the "new tape"—essentially, an archival system for cost-effectively storing petabytes or exabytes of data. But Hadoop has a much larger role to play in corporate computing environments, although its final trajectory is still unclear. Early adopters are using Hadoop primarily to stage Web log data, before parsing, aggregating, and moving it to a data warehouse where users can analyze the data with familiar SQL tools. But many also see Hadoop as a new analytical playground for data scientists with the data skills and programming savvy to explore Hadoop data and extract the proverbial needle from the data haystack.

Benefits. As an open source project hosted by the Apache Software Foundation, Hadoop brings three major benefits to the world of analytical processing:

- **LOW COST.** Because Hadoop is open source software that runs on commodity servers, it radically alters the financial equation for storing and processing large volumes of data—at least in terms of up-front software licensing costs. With Hadoop, organizations can finally store all the data they generate in its raw form without having to justify its business value up front or aggregate and move it to near-line or off-line storage.

- **AGILE.** Compared with relational databases, Hadoop does not require data developers to convert data to a specific format and schema (e.g., fields with fixed data types, lengths, labels and relationships) prior to loading data. Because it's a file system, Hadoop is a load-and-go environment that handles any data format, making it quick and easy vehicle for acquiring data. As a result, Hadoop encourages companies to explore data to determine whether it has any intrinsic value before they spend the time and money to load it into a data warehouse.

- **EXPRESSIVE.** Finally, Hadoop doesn't require users to use SQL to query data. Most application developers find SQL an alien programming environment and would rather use Java, Python, or other programming languages to access, manipulate, and analyze data. While SQL is good at many things, such as dimensional analysis, it is not as expressive as procedural code for certain types of analytical work, such as data mining, time-series analysis, or inter-row calculations.

Given these benefits, organizations are now finding creative ways to use Hadoop. For example, Vestas Wind Systems, a leading wind turbine maker, uses Hadoop to model larger volumes of weather data so that it can pinpoint the optimal placement for its wind turbines. And a financial services customer now runs its fraud models in Hadoop so that it can generate more accurate predictions against larger volumes of data.

Drawbacks. But Hadoop is not a data management or analytical panacea. It's essentially a 1.0 product that is missing many critical ingredients of an industrial-proof data processing environment. Namely, it's missing robust security, a universal metadata catalog, rich management utilities, and flexible application processing paradigms. Moreover, Hadoop is a batch-processing environment that doesn't support speed-of-thought and iterative querying. And although higher-level languages exist today, Hadoop requires generally data scientists who know how to write Java or other programs to access and manipulate Hadoop data, and these folks are in scarce supply.

In addition, to run a production-caliber Hadoop environment, you need to get software from a mishmash of Apache projects, which have colorful names like Flume, Sqoop, Oozie, Pig, Hive, and ZooKeeper. These independent projects often have competing functionality and separate release schedules, and they aren't always tightly integrated. And each project evolves rapidly. That's why there is a healthy market for Hadoop distributions that package these components into a reasonable set of implementable software. Because of the mishmash of code and missing enterprise features, the cost of putting Hadoop into production is high, although this will improve as the environment stabilizes and administrative and management utilities mature.

EVOLUTION

One good thing about Hadoop is that it is evolving fast. There are Apache projects to address most of Hadoop's shortcomings. One promising project is Hive, which provides SQL-like access to Hadoop. Another is HBase, a columnar database which overcomes Hadoop's latency issues and supports fast row-based reads and writes. Both create table-like structures on top of Hadoop files.

In addition, many commercial vendors have jumped into the fray, marrying SQL-based technology with open source software, turning Hadoop into a more corporate-friendly computing environment. Vendors such as Zettaset, EMC Greenplum, and Oracle have launched Hadoop appliances and seek to offer customers the best of both worlds. Many BI and data integration vendors now work seamlessly with Hadoop via application programming interfaces, and some, such as Talend, now run natively on Hadoop. Even Microsoft has jumped into the fray, offering a Hadoop port of Windows Server, an ODBC-to-Hive driver, and a new JavaScript framework for MapReduce that brings the masses of Windows developers into the world of Hadoop. The rapid merging of traditional SQL and Hadoop environments creates new possibilities for organizations to exploit all of their data for business gain.

Adoption rates. Leading-edge companies from a variety of industries have already implemented Hadoop, and many more are considering it. A survey of the BI Leadership Forum conducted in April, 2012 shows that 9% of organizations have implemented Hadoop, although only four percent have put it into production. Another 20% are experimenting with it, and 32% are considering it. On the downside, 38% have no plans to use Hadoop (see Figure 19-1).

FIGURE 19-1. ADOPTION OF HADOOP

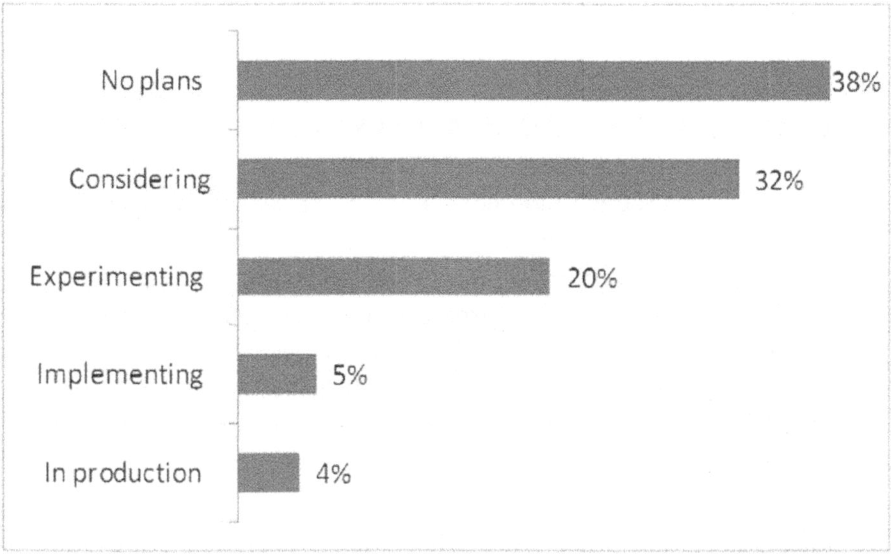

Based on 158 respondents, BI Leadership Forum, April, 2012 (www.bileadership.com).

Because of the enormous hype surrounding Hadoop, some analytical managers are asking whether Hadoop will replace their data warehouses and ETL tools. They wonder whether they should spend millions of dollars on a new analytical database if they can do the same processing without paying a dime in license costs. They want to know if they should spend hundreds of thousands of dollars on data integration tools if their data scientists can turn Hadoop into a huge data staging and transformation layer.

THE FUTURE IS CLOUDY

Right now, it's too early to divine the future of Hadoop and the big data movement and predict winners and losers. It's possible that in the future, all data management and analysis will run entirely on open source platforms and tools. But it's more likely that commercial vendors will co-opt (or outright buy) open source products and functionality and use them as sales pipelines for their commercial products. In the end, we'll probably get a mélange of open source and commercial capabilities. After all, the mainframe is still alive and well 30 years after its heyday. In IT, nothing ever dies; it just finds its niche in an evolutionary ecosystem.

COMMENTARY FROM ANALYTICAL LEADERS

TAYLOR: I have not spent a great deal of time or energy contemplating big data in the context of a Hadoop-oriented solution. Today we're primarily focused on structured data and managing the large volumes of data we already have. We have a lot of strategic things on our plate, right now. But I can see investigating the possibilities of Hadoop in the next 12 to 18 months once we gain traction for our new analytical platform and business unit.

THEARLING: Big data has a lot of potential. It gives us the ability to discern customer preferences and attitudes by watching actual behavior instead of analyzing market baskets or customer surveys. This behavioral data should be more accurate and less biased. For instance, Progressive Insurance sets your insurance premium based on your actual driving habits using a sensor that you install in your car. If you are a new customer, this enables Progressive to evaluate your risk much more accurately and can save the customer some money, too. If Progressive can effectively sift through all this data, they can create significant value by better understanding their customers.

But big data can be noisy. You can gather a lot of contextual data about customers but not get much value out of it. And in some cases, it may lead you astray. You need experts who can interpret all the signals correctly, like wilderness trackers who see a cracked twig or torn leaf in a trail and know who or what made those marks and when. Unfortunately, a lot of people can't recognize the signs and may misinterpret the signals. They see patterns in the data that don't really exist. So you need people who know how to interpret the signs and movements correctly, otherwise you'll find false patterns that can lead to poor business decisions.

O'CONNOR: Big data is absolutely critical to our strategy at Nokia. We are building products that make it easier to interact with the physical world, from personalized maps to augmented reality applications. Our success depends upon understanding how people, in general, interact with the world around them using anonymized traffic data, which is voluminous. So we need a big data strategy to deliver new insights and achieve our objectives.

One problem with having a big data strategy right now is that the Hadoop ecosystem is a moving target. It is new and changing quickly, sometimes every week or day. But we think it's the right direction for us. Right now, I spend a lot of development resources integrating our existing tools with Hadoop. However, we currently have a large development team in Bangalore, India that tackles this work, and we work closely with Cloudera and the Apache community to understand where the technology is going and make sure it's developed in a way that meets our needs. Every quarter we reassess our strategy and its impact on our analytical ecosystem.

Part of what I worry about is the "build it and they will come syndrome." If we put all the data in Hadoop, will people use it? Are we collecting the right data and combining and aggregating it in the right ways? So far, signals indicate that we are on the right track.

RUDIN: See Ken's entry in Chapters 15 and 17.

LEONARD: I'm a big believer in Hadoop. It's extremely flexible and we are finding all kinds of uses for it. I first used it in 2005 to sort, filter, and aggregate a five terabyte file on a 16-node cluster with help from a friend who knows Java. The job ran in just over 42 minutes and I was hooked. We primarily use it to do integration work, such as sorting and aggregating data. But occasionally, we use it for data exploration in concert with Pig and Hive. In essence, it's our data exploration sandbox.

What attracted me to Hadoop is the dexterity it provides architects. I can use my existing hardware and front-end tools. I can use it for almost any data processing work I have. I can change my architecture and infrastructure any time I want. It's a fluid environment. It doesn't bind to a proprietary schema.

We move all our data into Hadoop, which serves as our persistent storage area. This includes our electronic data interchange order data, call center data, our telemetric data from our trucks, and so on. We pull the data off our BizTalk messaging bus via Informatica adapters, which also match and clean data, where appropriate. We analyze data in Hadoop to identify patterns and outliers. But we also move data from Hadoop into our operational data store and data warehouse where users can access the data via OLAP cubes or dashboards.

One pattern we detected while analyzing Hadoop data was the lack of alignment between driver availability and timing of orders. Basically, orders were coming in when drivers weren't available and vice versa. So, we changed driver schedules to better align with the timing of orders. As a result, we can give drivers more time off and breaks without missing orders or underutilizing our fleet.

 **INGLE:** Our statisticians are evaluating Hadoop in a proof of concept led by our enterprise architecture team. The early feedback is that they feel Hadoop takes them back to the Dark Ages of computing where they have to submit a ticket that defines what data they want and then wait. The challenge with that process is that they don't always know what data they want until they see it, so they usually ask for everything.

Currently, the statisticians much prefer working with the data warehousing team, which gives them access to data at any stage in its lifecycle—from staging area to the data warehouse to reports—and partners with them to structure the data into an ideal format for analytical modeling. The statisticians' preference for the data warehouse may change over time as they explore the capability and uses of Hadoop.

In addition, Hadoop would have a significant impact on our technical architecture and require us to hire people with specialized skills to set up, optimize, and maintain a Hadoop cluster of any real size. However, I know that new tools and extensions are making Hadoop easier to work with. That said, I have not ruled it out as an option and continue to keep an eye on it should our current ecosystem struggle to meet our needs.

COLSON: Hadoop plays a vital role in an analytics environment. It serves as the persistence and compute layer for big data – the data that has high-velocity, high-volume, and varying structure. These qualities differentiate big data from data traditionally handled by relational databases. It's important to note that Hadoop is not a replacement for the relational database, but rather a much needed complement.

In this model Hadoop takes on more of the warehouse role while the relational database behaves more like a mart. The mart designation does not mean its scope has been reduced to supporting a single department; the mart still takes on an enterprise scope. However, the designation of 'mart' means that the relational database will not have all the data. It may have only the most relevant and anticipated data—and sometimes only in aggregate form. This subset of data is well-vetted, well-modeled, and well-tuned which makes it well-suited for a relational database.

By contrast Hadoop better handles the voluminous data that is more varied in structure. It typically contains the super set of event data that is logged directly from operational systems in its rawest form. And, unlike the relational database where a schema must be defined before any data can be loaded, Hadoop allows you to structure the data later—at query time. This allows you to be flexible and fluid in how you load and acquire data. Sometimes you might simply want to explore data before deciding what to do with it. And that's the beauty of Hadoop. There are virtually no coordination costs to putting more data into it. In many cases the structure is imposed only at query time using MapReduce directly or higher-level languages like Pig or Hive. You can then process and export the data, filtering, aggregating and restructuring it to a format suitable for the relational database.

This tiered environment, where you use Hadoop for the big data and a relational database as a mart, leverages the strengths of each technology. Hadoop is geared to analytic batch processing of variably structured data, while relational databases are ideal for running fast, interactive queries against structured data. They are perfect complements.

SUMMARY

Big data has become synonymous with Hadoop. Although Hadoop advocates believe the technology will soon subsume the data warehouse and its SQL artifacts, the more likely scenario is that Hadoop will function as a staging area and archive that complements the data warehouse. Over time, Hadoop will likely acquire a greater share of reporting and analysis tasks, especially those that run against unstructured and semi-structured data. Of course, predicting the future is never easy, but in the next chapter, our analytical leaders take out their crystal balls and try to divine the future of analytics.

CHAPTER 20

WHAT IS THE FUTURE
OF ANALYTICS?

Our analytical leaders found it difficult to predict the future of analytics. Ken Rudin said we have enough technology and need to spend time digesting and making more effective use of it. Tim Leonard believes the next user interface is voice-activated, allowing business users to generate queries by speaking into their iPhones or iPads. He also believes Hadoop will consume the data warehouse and most analytics will run on mobile devices. Kurt Thearling believes we are on the verge of sensor revolution but companies will be challenged to process the data in a timely fashion and do anything meaningful with it. Amy O'Connor believes the time is right for companies to appoint Chief Data Officers, among other things. And Eric Colson sees a future in which applications link dynamically to external data used for analytical purposes.

COMPUTE PLATFORMS

When I look into my crystal ball, it's clear that new computing platforms are driving new rounds of innovation in the analytics market. These innovations include Hadoop, mobile devices, and cloud computing. Each new computing platform stirs up the marketplace and creates new winners and losers.

As we discussed in the last chapter, Hadoop is the hottest platform in town, right now, but mobile computing is fast behind. As Tim Leonard points out, we're in the midst of a mobile revolution, and this shows no signs of abating. Mobile computing has given many analytics programs a major shot in the arm.

Cloud computing offers potential for analytics, but is evolving more slowly. That's largely because analytics is hard to package as a generic application, which is critical to delivering the economies of scale required by software-as-a-service vendors. Analytics is better suited to a platform-as-a-service offering that enables customers to create custom applications in the cloud. But here, the cloud is neither inexpensive nor quick to deploy, which minimizes its appeal for some. Nonetheless, I believe analytics in the cloud is inevitable.

NEW INTELLIGENCES

Beyond new computing platforms, the future of analytics will continue its relentless march toward delivering the right information to the right people at the right time. Unfortunately, for more than two decades, analytical professionals have tried to manage diverse types of business users, workloads, and data in the same architecture, often with disappointing results. The problem is that analytics is a broad domain.

In the next decade, analytical leaders will adopt new thinking and approaches. They will break away from the "one size fits all" architecture of the past. To meet emerging business demands, they will manage multiple domains of intelligence and their associated architectures, each of which is optimized for different classes of users and workloads. With a flexible approach to data architecture, analytical leaders will be able to better meet the information requirements of all its business users.

FOUR INTELLIGENCES

Figure 20-1 depicts the future of analytics at a high level. It defines four distinct domains of "intelligence" and maps them to end-user tools, design environments, and architectures. All four environments are designed to support reporting and analysis applications, depicted in the middle of the diagram. We discussed two of these domains in the last chapter—business intelligence and analytics intelligence—and their impact on the emerging analytical ecosystem. (Figure 17-2 depicts the reference architecture that implements the analytical framework in figure 20-1.)

FIGURE 20-1. A FRAMEWORK FOR THE FUTURE OF ANALYTICS

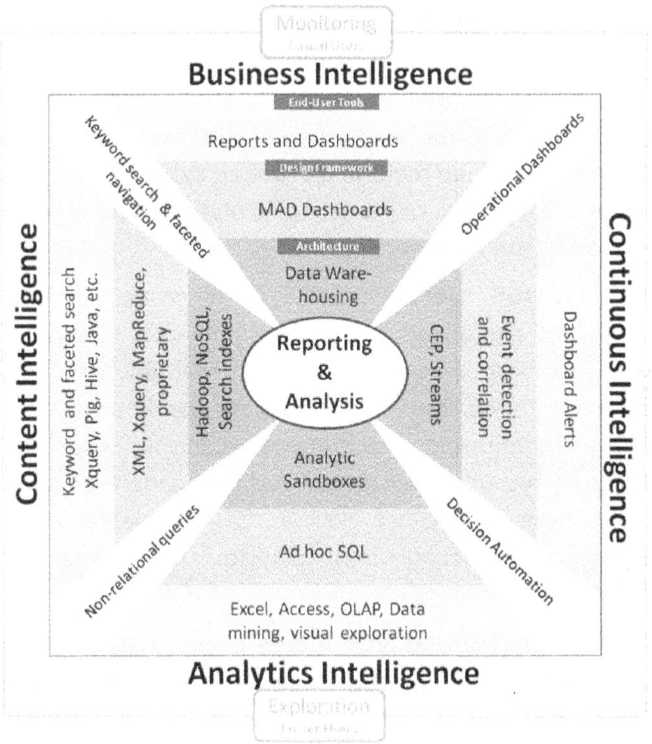

Business intelligence, with its reliance on data warehousing, will no longer dominate the analytical landscape in the future. It will be accompanied by three other intelligences, which are manifested in the analytical ecosystem, described in the previous chapter.

The four intelligences are:

- **BUSINESS INTELLIGENCE.** Addresses the needs of "casual users"—executives, managers, front-line workers, customers, and suppliers. It delivers reports, dashboards, and scorecards that are tailored to each user's role and populated with metrics aligned with strategic objectives and goals. This "top-down" driven environment is powered by a classic data warehousing architecture that consolidates enterprise data and enforces information consistency by transforming shared data into a common data model (i.e., schema) and BI semantic layer (i.e., metadata.)

- **ANALYTICS INTELLIGENCE.** Provides "power users"—that is, business analysts, analytical modelers, and data scientists—with ad hoc access to any data inside or outside the enterprise, so they can answer unanticipated business questions and run complex analytical models against all the data. Traditionally, this type of "bottom-up" analysis has been done in spreadsheets, desktop databases, OLAP tools, and data mining workbenches. To make analysts full-fledged members of the analytical ecosystem, organizations are increasingly creating analytical sandboxes within or adjacent to the data warehouse.

- **CONTINUOUS INTELLIGENCE.** Automates the collection, monitoring, and analysis of high-velocity data to support operational processes. It ranges from near real-time delivery of information (i.e., hours to minutes) in a data warehousing environment to tens of thousands of events per second in a specialized event streaming system that collects machine-generated data coming from sensors and other devices. These event-based systems correlate events across time and systems and trigger alerts when predefined conditions are met.

- **CONTENT INTELLIGENCE.** Gives business users the ability to access and analyze unstructured data (e.g., text, audio, video, images) and semi-structured data (e.g., documents, Web pages, Web logs, email messages, social media feeds.) Content intelligence uses a variety of technologies and techniques to capture and query non-traditional data types. These systems include Hadoop, NoSQL databases, search technology, graphing systems, semantic technology, and so on. These systems also can store and query structured data, creating a universal data management system that gives users one place to access all data in an organization.

Overlay Dimension. The framework also shows one overlay dimension that runs vertically. The top half of the diagram (like the top half of the analytical ecosystem in Chapter 17) represents top down analytics, while the bottom half represents bottom-up analytics.

In top-down "monitoring" environments, casual users know what data they want to look at in advance, and the IT team bakes those requirements into various information models that govern what data gets displayed and how it is accessed. This describes traditional data warehousing and BI environments and dashboards created with Hadoop, search technologies, or CEP engines.

The bottom half of the diagram represents exploratory environments in which users run ad hoc queries against various sources of data to answer new and unanticipated questions. Because the questions keep changing and data attributes are volatile, it's nearly impossible to model the data in advance using traditional data approaches. Typically, power users use spreadsheets and desktop databases to collect, integrate, and analyze structured data; and they use Hadoop, NoSQL databases, and search technology to analyze unstructured data.

Intelligence Intersections. The intersections between the four intelligences create an opportunity for high-value applications. Blending the best of two domains delivers sizable business value. For example, *operational dashboards,* which sit at the intersection of business intelligence and continuous intelligence, deliver the highest value of any type of dashboard (i.e., operational, tactical, and strategic), according to my research. Similarly, *decision automation,* which sits at the intersection of continuous intelligence and analytical intelligence, embeds analytical models into process flows, allowing organizations to automate high-value interactions.

The ability to *query non-relational data* sits between analytics intelligence and content intelligence, giving users access to 80% of corporate data that previously wasn't accessible in traditional data warehouses. Finally, *BI search tools* sit at the intersection of content intelligence and business intelligence. They enable casual users to generate queries and reports by typing words into a search box, which makes it easy for them to explore data when they need true ad hoc capabilities.

The message behind the analytical framework depicted above is that you can't shoehorn all analytical activities into a single environment. Rather than provide a single architecture and toolset, analytical professionals need to create an analytical ecosystem that supports multiple reporting and analysis environments. There may be multiple teams managing these environments, but ideally they work closely together to establish standard data definitions and data flows.

COMMENTARY FROM ANALYTICAL LEADERS

RUDIN: We have more technology than we know how to use effectively today. Therefore, new technology will only help at the margins. The biggest advances will come from people who figure out how to apply the technology they already have to deliver real business value. The companies that have been most successful with analytics started with a shoestring budget. When I joined Zynga, we didn't have any money to buy database licenses, so we ran our games on hundreds of MySQL databases, and we ran our analytics on discarded game servers. Since then, we've only bought two pieces of commercial software (Vertica and Tableau) and we've either built or leveraged open source technology for the rest.

I also think business intelligence will move from being a discrete business unit or function to an embedded one. To make actionable information part of the business culture, organizations will discover they need to embed business analysts and report developers in the business units and have them sit side by side with the business people they support.

LEONARD: I believe the user interface for computers will move from keyboard to touch screen to voice activation. Users will always be able to type or touch, but increasingly, we'll see users interact with their computers via intelligent, voice recognition software backed by a NoSQL knowledgebase, like Apple's Siri or IBM's Watson. In the analytics world, you'll say "What are sales data for region X" and you'll hear an answer and see a chart.

Going forward, people will have less time and inclination to open a dashboard and look at it. We're in a mobile workplace wearing multiple hats so our data needs are generally broad, not deep. I can see U.S. Xpress executives asking their computers, "How many drivers today were not dispatched?" And they hear and see the answer. Of course, that impels them to ask other questions, such as: "Of the 23 drivers who weren't dispatched today, how many scored below average in employee satisfaction?" We are three to five years away from achieving this vision, which ultimately blends structured and unstructured data behind a voice-activated user interface.

Also, I believe Hadoop will eventually consume the data warehouse. In five to seven years, Hadoop clusters will run the data warehouse and we'll be able to get rid of our current relational databases. In fact, we'll do all our processing in Hadoop, both analytics and transactions. All the ETL and BI tools have connectors to Hadoop right now, so I'd be worried if I was Teradata, Microsoft, Oracle, or IBM. Today, Hadoop is a batch processing environment, but it won't stay that way for long.

The pace of technology innovation and adoption keeps increasing. We are on the cusp of a perfect storm. Hadoop will evolve much faster than prior generations of technologies. People shouldn't be content to be late adopters or laggards with the technology. It only took me two years to adopt the entire Hadoop architecture and put it into production. Now everybody is working with it.

THEARLING: We are about to be flooded with data. Some of this data will be the crumbs left over from activities we already track. But some of the data will be new, collected for the first time as technology moves forward. We are entering the age of the sensor. We are starting to see sensors in phones, automobiles, truck engines, electric meters, pipelines, buildings, bridges, roads, and agricultural fields.

We'll eventually have medical devices inserted in our bodies to monitor our health and sensors in our lawns that connect to our sprinkler systems. Data collection will be everywhere.

The key question is whether we have the ability to do something constructive with this flood of sensor data. With telehealth, we'll have a lot of medical devices in the home that can check blood pressure, glucose, and weight and send results to a medical provider, but will anyone be looking at this data? And will the data be presented in a way that makes it easy to identify anomalies and patterns? Thanks to smart utility meter technology, utilities will collect a lot of information about energy consumption. But many utilities are not equipped to handle this data onslaught. They're simply collecting the data because a public utility commission told them to. If they have the know-how and infrastructure, they might be able to do wonderful things with the data, like create time-of-day rates. But that requires a shift in the business that is beyond simply collecting the data.

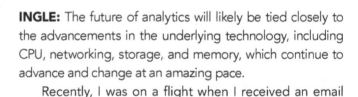

INGLE: The future of analytics will likely be tied closely to the advancements in the underlying technology, including CPU, networking, storage, and memory, which continue to advance and change at an amazing pace.

Recently, I was on a flight when I received an email from my wife explaining that my 8-year old son was in tears because he was about to go to the orthodontist to get braces. So, I picked up my iPad and called him using Facetime and tried to calm him down. Here I am, sitting 35,000 feet in the air, chatting by video with my son who is in San Diego. Literally, the sky is the limit for what technology can do in the future.

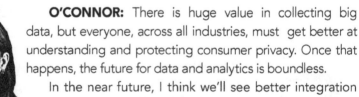

O'CONNOR: There is huge value in collecting big data, but everyone, across all industries, must get better at understanding and protecting consumer privacy. Once that happens, the future for data and analytics is boundless.

In the near future, I think we'll see better integration among Hadoop tools within the open source community and between Hadoop and SQL-based tools. This integration is desperately needed. We'll also see the emergence of query and analysis tools that mere mortals can use to query Hadoop. Better yet, I hope we see tools that somehow incorporate the curiosity of data scientists so other analysts can mine data more effectively. Finally, I believe the role of Chief Data Officer will become prevalent as organizations recognize the importance of analytics and data.

 **COLSON:** I think we'll see start to see analytics that extends beyond the walls of the enterprise. Many organizations use external sources already, integrating data from third parties such as Twitter, Facebook, and Google Trends. However, the current approach is to take the external data and make it internal. That is, the data is copied into the enterprise before it is used for analytic processing.

In the future, I suspect we will consider prominent reference data as a virtual extension to our data warehouses. In this way, data can be linked and shared across organizations and applications. For example, Facebook data may make up parts of a customer dimension. And, Wikipedia may become reference data for other objects. And, rather than copy the data into the enterprise data warehouse, we'll leave it in place and call or join to it as needed. Such distributed reference data will be an application of Berners-Lee's *Semantic Web* to analytics and data warehousing.

Achieving this aspirational vision will result in full acceptance of semi-structured data—no more fixed schemas. That is, reliance on third parties to manage this reference data will force us to be more flexible with structure. The reference data will provide an arbitrary and evolving number of attributes for each entity from which developers can access as they wish. This will include descriptive attributes as well as denormalizations of factual data. For example, a celebrity may be unambiguously identified by Wikipedia article ID number and we'll describe him or her using the number of Tweets or Facebook "Likes" he or she has garnered. All this reference data will be in a format readable by both machines and humans (say JSON or XML) and accessible via open URLs.

We'll continue to produce analytics for human consumption, but there will more and more innovation around machine consumption. Increasingly, machines will digest and take action on the data, making decisions on our behalf. We do this today with algorithms, but we are only scratching the surface in the amount of information being leveraged. In the future we'll squeeze more and more value out of every piece of data we can capture. Each will be used to inform just marginally better, but in aggregate the data and analytics will move us to unprecedented levels of efficiency.

As more and more value is generated from the actions taken, the line between data developers and application developers might begin to blur. With less reliance on central data architectures, data developers can move into functional areas, such as product, engineering, and marketing. Skills in higher-level languages like SQL and packaged enterprise solutions will be commoditized or too restrictive. The market will demand the flexibility and innovation that comes with more robust coding skills like Python. And, as always, the individual who can conceive of and implement creative data solutions will thrive in the amount of business value they can deliver.

 **TAYLOR:** The potential for analytics in healthcare is boundless. The entire industry is quickly becoming more sophisticated and complex, so organizations that generate proactive insights will have a competitive advantage. Looking in the rear view mirror is no longer good enough.

Health insurance plans (payers) typically house tremendous amounts of structured and unstructured data and many have done a good job using this data to run their core operations. But now, business models are changing due to healthcare reform and competitive pressures. To adapt to these changes, healthcare payers need to improve the way they organize and analyze data.

For example, more payers will shift from employer-sponsored health plans to direct-to-consumer plans with the advent of health care exchanges and subsidized individual premiums. This change will require payers to "know" their individual members and prospective customers, including such things as their willingness to participate in health and wellness programs. Organizations that have invested in integrated data and analytics will have an advantage here.

Service providers (physicians, hospitals, etc.) also need better data and analytic capabilities as the industry moves from fee-for-service payments to new models that reward providers for patient outcomes. They need to monitor a host of metrics around preventive care, surgical outcomes, hospital re-admissions, and so on. They also need to adapt to new financial risk sharing models between payers and providers.

SUMMARY

Although analytical leaders offer various views of the future of analytics, it's clear that innovation is the watchword in this field. As companies discover the power of data and analytics, they will devise ways to fully exploit the technologies and analytical skills they have inhouse as well as employ new technologies to generate valuable new insights and actions.

APPENDIX

RECOMMENDED READING

Analytical professionals are voracious readers and learners. Their appetite for knowledge comes largely from the rapid pace of technological advancement as well as their continually shifting responsibilities, which require them to quickly master new technologies and skills. Books are the quickest and cheapest way to acquire knowledge fast so it's informative to hear what our analytical leaders are reading.

RECOMMENDATIONS FROM ANALYTICAL LEADERS

 **ECKERSON:** I'd recommend *How We Decide* by Jonah Lehrer (2009). Reviewing the latest in neurological and behavioral research, Lehrer shows that humans have an emotional brain that plays a critical role in decision making. Lehrer argues that the best decision makers know when to listen to their emotions and when to override them. He also provides convincing evidence that the best way a person can improve their decision making and performance is by intensely studying their mistakes and learning from them.

Another terrific book that pulls back the veil on human and organizational behavior is *The Power of Habit: Why We Do What We Do in Life and Business* by Charles Duhigg (2012). This book examines the habit cycle: cue→behavior→reward, and how advertisers and marketers use it to sell more products, organizations use it effect cultural change and train workers. From an analytics perspective, there are great examples from Alcoa, Starbucks, and Target about how managing habits are the key any change management initiative. In fact, the section on Target reveals the eerie power of analytical models to predict customer behavior.

Along the same vein, a classic book is *The Fifth Discipline: The Art and Practice of The Learning Organization* (1990) by Peter Senge. The book provides a recipe for empowering organizations to achieve breakthrough performance. At its core, the book teaches the reader about systems theory and how to apply it to unravel dysfunctional organizational behaviors. But it's also about personal mastery, teamwork, and visioning, and mental models. It's thought provocative and compelling.

I'd also read *Data Mining Techniques for Marketing, Sales, and Customer Support* by Michal J.A. Berry and Gordon Linhoff (1997) This book explains data mining techniques and methods in language that mere mortals can understand. It's a good starting point for venturing into the world of machine learning.

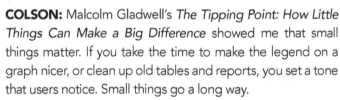

COLSON: Malcolm Gladwell's *The Tipping Point: How Little Things Can Make a Big Difference* showed me that small things matter. If you take the time to make the legend on a graph nicer, or clean up old tables and reports, you set a tone that users notice. Small things go a long way.

Eliyahu Goldratt's *The Goal: A Process of Ongoing Improvement* shaped my thinking on spanners—data developers who build an entire analytical solution from scratch. The book is a novel about a harried plant manager who learns how to improve process efficiency by applying Goldratt's Theory of Constraints. The theory shows how small fluctuations within interdependent systems become additive, turning into major bottlenecks. If you remove system dependencies, you improve process efficiencies.

From Gladwell's *What the Dog Saw: And Other Adventures,* I learned the importance of context when managing people. For example, until you step inside the shoes of a data developer and see what makes them tick, you can't understand what motivates them. Without this context, you end up putting people in the wrong positions.

Along the same lines, Daniel H. Pink's *Drive: The Surprising Truth About What Motivates Us* is equally powerful. It shows that people aren't motivated by money as much as autonomy, mastery, and purpose. One reason I like the spanner approach is that it aligns with these concepts. Spanners have more autonomy, mastery, and purpose, and thus are more productive and happier at what they do.

I also benefited a lot from Richard Dawkins' book, *The Greatest Show on Earth: The Evidence for Evolution*, which examines the merits of evolution and intelligent design. This book helped validate my principle of "eventual cohesion" in which you evolve your data models and architectures incrementally, and sometimes independently, and then align them after the fact.

For example, Dawkins shows how creatures evolve gradually using the process of natural selection. Rather than create a perfect design upfront, evolution makes many small changes along the way. This doesn't lead to the perfect design, but it enables the organism to adapt to changes. For example, if you designed a giraffe from scratch, you would not make its laryngeal nerve take a 15-foot detour down to its chest and back again. But, according to Dawkins, that's what happened to giraffes since they evolved from deer-like animals with shorter necks.

However, at some point, the marginal cost of an evolutionary design outweighs the advantages gained through adaption, and you have to start over. Dawkins admits this should occur in evolution but almost never does because the cost of a major upheaval is rarely worth the advantages. However, in analytics, we often need to reset or "cohere" our data models or applications so they integrate and provide a solid foundation for future growth. This major overhaul is called 'punctuated change.' For example, last summer, we decided to wipe out our data model and start afresh because it had so many patches that slowed it down and made it hard to work with.

 **TAYLOR:** I am a big believer in the principles outlined in books by Marcus Buckingham: *First Break all the Rules: What the World's Great Managers Do Differently* and *Now, Discover Your Strengths*. The books contradict the prevailing thinking in most human resources departments. For instance, one major tenet is that instead of grooming people for jobs, you should put them in positions that align with their natural

talents. In other words, don't force people into positions that don't match their abilities. But that happens all the time. John Kotter's *Leading Change* has also influenced the way I've handled change management issues within Blue KC.

INGLE: I make everyone who joins my team read *The Five Dysfunctions of a Team* by Patrick Lencioni. He lays out a simple, easy to understand, model of what makes a team effective. He says the foundation is trust. Without trust, team members won't risk saying what they think and there won't be healthy debate or conflict. We spend a lot of time focusing on teamwork here. It's a key to our success. (See Ingle's commentary in Chapter 9.)

RUDIN: I don't have a book to recommend, but many years ago I saw Stephen Few present, and he said that the primary purpose of charts and dashboards is to get people to act. It's not about clever graphical presentations of data or figuring out how to cram as many data points as possible on screen. It's about getting people to act. That helped define my philosophy that the value of analytics comes from changing people's behavior. If you present incredible insights to people, but their behavior doesn't change in any way, then by definition, you've added no value. That's been a guiding philosophy of how I manage analytics teams. I don't care how cool your insight is—if it didn't impact the company, then it didn't add any value.

Stephen Few is a widely regarded expert on visualization techniques for displaying business information. He has written several books: *Show Me the Numbers: Designing Tables and Graphs to Enlighten, Information Dashboard Design: The Effective Visual Communication of Data,* and *Now You See It: Simple Visualization Techniques for Quantitative Analysis.*

THEARLING: My favorite book about data is Edward Tufte's *Envisioning Information.* Tufte's book shows how to present data in a clear, concise way so that you can get your point across. He exhorts people to present information in a straightforward and honest way. Besides being a fantastic book about the topic of data, it is also one of the most beautiful books I have ever seen. The graphic design, layout, and use of type are extraordinary. The book is a great example of how to visually share information and Tufte has had a huge impact on how I approach working with data.

 **O'CONNOR:** *Freakonomics* is a great read for anyone wondering about the usefulness of disparate datasets. The authors Levitt and Dubner mine diverse combinations of data, and come up with unique perspectives on the world. Thinking out-of-the-box is important if you want to drive the most value from your data – and this book provides some entertaining examples of just such thinking.

I also recommend reading reports on big data and analytics from McKinsey & Company, Accenture, and MIT Sloan School of Management.